DEDALO AGENCY

IRELAND

Travel guide

HOW TO PLAN
A TRIP TO IRELAND
WITH BEST TIPS
FOR FIRST-TIMERS

Edited by: Domenico Russo and Francesco Umbria
Design e layout: Giorgia Ragona
Book series: Journey Joy

IRELAND
Travel guide

Index
. . . .

Introduction

Welcome to Ireland, the Emerald Isle, where every bend in the road reveals a landscape steeped in myth, history, and breathtaking beauty. This enchanting island offers more than just its famous green hills and dramatic coastlines; it's a vibrant tapestry of culture, music, folklore, and hospitality that beckons travelers from around the globe. Whether you're planning your first visit or looking to immerse yourself deeply in its rich heritage, this guide is crafted to help you navigate Ireland's diverse regions and unique charms with ease and delight.

Ireland is a land where ancient legends and modern life blend seamlessly, making it a perfect destination for both short explorative trips and extended cultural sojourns. The island's allure extends beyond its iconic landmarks and scenic vistas; it's a hub of artistic expression, culinary delights, and welcoming communities that cater to a wide array of interests and passions. In this guide, we will journey through the heart of Ireland's most beloved regions, starting with the vibrant capital of Dublin. Here, history and contemporary culture coexist harmoniously, from the grandeur of Trinity College and the Book of Kells to the lively atmosphere of Temple Bar. We'll explore the cultural treasures and historic landmarks that define Dublin, setting the stage for your Irish adventure.

Next, we'll take you along the Wild Atlantic Way, a spectacular coastal route that showcases Ireland's rugged beauty and natural wonders. From the towering Cliffs of Moher and the charming town of Dingle to the scenic Ring of Kerry and the mystical Skellig Michael, this route promises awe-inspiring vistas and unforgettable experiences.

The Ancient East offers a deep dive into Ireland's storied past, with visits to medieval castles, monastic ruins, and prehistoric tombs. Discover the spiritual serenity of Glendalough, the medieval charm of Kilkenny, and the historical intrigue of Newgrange. This region is a treasure trove of historical landmarks that tell the tale of Ireland's rich and complex history.

Northern Ireland combines stunning landscapes with profound historical significance. Explore the natural marvel of the Giant's Causeway, walk the historic walls of Derry, and visit the Titanic Belfast museum. The region's blend of natural beauty and historical depth provides a unique and enriching travel experience.

Beyond the well-known attractions, Ireland is dotted with hidden gems waiting to be discovered. From the lesser-known beauty of Burren National Park and the serene Glenveagh National Park to the towering Slieve League Cliffs and the enchanting Kylemore Abbey, these hidden treasures offer a deeper connection to Ireland's untouched landscapes.

Irish culture is vibrant and welcoming, deeply rooted in its traditions and everyday life. Experience traditional Irish music sessions, Gaelic games, and lively festivals that celebrate the island's heritage. Delve into Irish folklore, visit literary landmarks, and immerse yourself in the warm hospitality that Ireland is renowned for.

The island's culinary journey is equally enticing, with flavors that range from hearty traditional breakfasts to the freshest seafood. Discover where to enjoy classic Irish stews, artisan cheeses, and freshly baked bread. Ireland's pub culture is an essential part of this experience, offering everything from classic pub grub to gourmet dishes.

Practical travel tips will guide you in planning your visit, choosing the best times to explore, and finding the right accommodations. Learn about transportation options, budgeting tips, health and safety considerations, and cultural etiquette. These insights will ensure a seamless and enjoyable travel experience.

Immerse yourself in Ireland's rich cultural heritage with ten must-have experiences, from attending local festivals and exploring whiskey distilleries to participating in traditional music sessions and Gaelic games. This guide will help you connect deeply with the cultural fabric of Ireland.

Whether you're planning a short visit or an extended stay, this guide offers detailed itineraries to help you make the most of your time in Ireland. Explore Dublin's attractions, the scenic routes of the Wild Atlantic Way, the historical sites of the Ancient East, and the natural beauty of Northern Ireland. These itineraries are designed to provide a balanced and enriching travel experience.

Your journey through Ireland is more than just a vacation; it's an opportunity to connect with a land of stories, beauty, and warmth. Let this guide be your trusted companion, helping you uncover the essence of Ireland at every turn. From its bustling cities to its tranquil countryside, Ireland welcomes you with open arms and a heart full of history and culture. Prepare to be enchanted, inspired, and transformed by the magic of the Emerald Isle.

CHAPTER 1:
Dublin
· · · · · · · · · · ·

Dublin, the vibrant heart of Ireland, is a city where history, culture, and modernity blend seamlessly. As you stroll through its cobblestone streets, you'll encounter a rich tapestry of ancient landmarks, bustling markets, and contemporary attractions. Dublin's charm lies in its ability to offer something for everyone, from literary enthusiasts and history buffs to foodies and nightlife seekers. This chapter will guide you through the highlights of Dublin, providing a blend of historical insights and practical tips to help you make the most of your visit.

Dublin is not just a city; it's a living, breathing embodiment of Irish heritage. Founded by the Vikings and shaped by centuries of history, Dublin's streets are lined with stories waiting to be discovered. Whether you're marveling at the medieval architecture of Dublin Castle, delving into the literary legacy of James Joyce, or simply enjoying a pint at a traditional pub, you'll find that every corner of Dublin has a tale to tell. In this guide, we'll explore some of the city's most iconic attractions and hidden gems, offering a comprehensive overview that will enhance your travel experience.

Our journey through Dublin begins with its most notable landmarks, including Trinity College and the Book of Kells, the Guinness Storehouse, and St. Patrick's Cathedral. Each site offers a unique glimpse into Dublin's past and present, providing a foundation upon which to build your exploration of this captivating city. We'll also delve into the vibrant neighborhoods and cultural hubs that define Dublin's contemporary character, from the artistic enclave of Temple Bar to the serene expanses of Phoenix Park. By the end of this chapter, you'll have a well-rounded understanding of Dublin's historical significance and modern allure, ready to embark on your own Dublin adventure.

Trinity College and the Book of Kells

Trinity College, founded in 1592 by Queen Elizabeth I, is Ireland's oldest university and a cornerstone of Dublin's historical and cultural landscape. The college's stately Georgian architecture and tranquil quadrangles create an atmosphere of scholarly reflection, inviting visitors to step back in time. The crown jewel of Trinity College is undoubtedly the Book of Kells, an illuminated manuscript created by Celtic monks around the year 800 AD. This masterpiece of medieval art is housed in the Old Library, whose Long Room is a stunning sight with its barrel-vaulted ceiling and towering bookcases.

Visitors to Trinity College can explore the Old Library and view the Book of Kells, which is renowned for its intricate illustrations and vibrant colors. The exhibit provides insight into the book's creation and significance, offering a deeper appreciation for this ancient artifact. The Long Room, often described as one of the most beautiful libraries in the world, is home to over 200,000 of the library's oldest books and is a highlight of any visit to Trinity College.

For practical tips, it's best to book tickets online in advance to avoid long queues, especially during peak tourist season. Guided tours are available and highly recommended, as they provide rich historical context and fascinating anecdotes about the college and its treasures. Plan to spend at least an hour exploring the library and its exhibits, and don't forget to take a stroll through the college's picturesque grounds, which offer a peaceful retreat in the heart of the city.

Guinness Storehouse

The Guinness Storehouse, located in the heart of the St. James's Gate Brewery, is one of Dublin's most popular tourist attractions and a must-visit for beer enthusiasts. Opened in 2000, the Storehouse is a seven-story visitor experience dedicated to the history and heritage of Guinness, Ireland's iconic stout. The building itself is designed in the shape of a giant pint glass, and as you ascend through the floors, you'll learn about the brewing process, the history of the brand, and its global impact.

The tour begins on the ground floor with an introduction to the four ingredients of beer – water, barley, hops, and yeast – and progresses through various interactive exhibits. Highlights include the Cooperage, where you can learn about the craft of barrel-making, and the Advertising Floor, which showcases decades of iconic Guinness ads. The journey culminates in the Gravity Bar on the top floor, where you can enjoy a complimentary pint of Guinness while taking in panoramic views of Dublin.

To make the most of your visit, consider booking your tickets online to benefit from discounted rates and skip-the-line access. Allow at least two hours to explore the Storehouse fully, and take advantage of the guided tours and tasting sessions offered throughout the day. The Gravity Bar can get crowded, so aim to visit early in the morning or late in the afternoon for the best experience. Don't forget to visit the gift shop on your way out to pick up unique Guinness memorabilia.

Dublin Castle

Dublin Castle, with its origins dating back to the 13th century, is a historic landmark that has played a central role in Ireland's history. Originally built as a defensive fortification by the Normans, it has since evolved into a complex of buildings that reflect various architectural styles, from medieval to Georgian. The castle has served multiple purposes over the centuries, including as a military fortress, a royal residence, and the seat of British administration in Ireland. Today, it is a major tourist attraction and a venue for state functions and official events.

Visitors to Dublin Castle can explore a number of fascinating sites within the complex, including the State Apartments, which are richly decorated and used for important state functions, and the Chapel Royal, a stunning example of Gothic Revival architecture. The medieval undercroft reveals the remnants of the original Viking and Norman structures, offering a glimpse into the castle's ancient past. The Chester Beatty Library, located on the castle grounds, houses a remarkable collection of manuscripts, rare books, and artworks from around the world, further enhancing the cultural experience of a visit to Dublin Castle.

For practical tips, consider joining a guided tour to gain a deeper understanding of the castle's history and significance. Tours typically last about an hour and cover all major parts of the complex. It's advisable to check the schedule for any state events that might limit access to certain areas. The castle is centrally located, making it easy to incorporate into a day of sight-seeing in Dublin. After your visit, take a leisurely walk around the Dubh Linn Gardens behind the castle, a tranquil spot perfect for relaxation.

St. Patrick's Cathedral

St. Patrick's Cathedral, the largest cathedral in Ireland, is one of Dublin's most iconic landmarks. Founded in 1191, it has been at the heart of Ireland's religious and cultural life for over 800 years. The cathedral is dedicated to St. Patrick, the patron saint of Ireland, and is built on the site where it is believed he baptized converts to Christianity. The Gothic architecture of the cathedral, with its impressive spire and stunning stained-glass windows, creates an awe-inspiring atmosphere that draws visitors from around the world.

Inside the cathedral, you'll find a wealth of historical artifacts and memorials, including the tomb of Jonathan Swift, the famous author of "Gulliver's Travels" and former Dean of St. Patrick's. The Lady Chapel, the Choir, and the Nave are beautifully adorned and steeped in history. The cathedral also hosts a number of cultural and religious events throughout the year, adding to its vibrant role in the community. The adjacent St. Patrick's Park offers a peaceful retreat and features a statue of St. Patrick and an ornamental fountain.

When visiting St. Patrick's Cathedral, it's recommended to purchase tickets in advance to avoid long queues. Audio guides are available for those who prefer to explore at their own pace, while guided tours provide in-depth historical insights. The cathedral is open daily, but hours may vary on weekends and during special events, so it's best to check the schedule beforehand. After your visit, take some time to enjoy St. Patrick's Park, which offers beautiful views of the cathedral and a serene environment for reflection.

Temple Bar District

The Temple Bar District is Dublin's cultural quarter, known for its vibrant nightlife, artistic vibe, and historic charm. Located on the south bank of the River Liffey, Temple Bar is a lively area filled with pubs, restaurants, galleries, and cultural institutions. The district's narrow, cobblestone streets are home to some of the city's most popular attractions, making it a must-visit for anyone looking to experience Dublin's dynamic atmosphere. Whether you're seeking live music, unique shops, or simply a lively place to enjoy a pint, Temple Bar has something to offer.

Temple Bar is famous for its traditional Irish pubs, where you can enjoy live music sessions and a hearty meal. The area also hosts a number of markets, including the Temple Bar Food Market, which offers a variety of local and artisanal foods, and the Temple Bar Book Market, perfect for book lovers and collectors. Cultural venues such as the Irish Film Institute, the Project Arts Centre, and the Temple Bar Gallery and Studios add to the district's artistic appeal, providing a rich array of performances, exhibitions, and screenings.

To make the most of your visit to Temple Bar, plan to explore the area both during the day and at night, as it offers different experiences. Daytime visits allow you to enjoy the markets and cultural attractions, while the nighttime atmosphere is perfect for experiencing Dublin's famous pub culture. Be prepared for crowds, especially on weekends, and consider making reservations at popular restaurants and pubs. Temple Bar is easily accessible on foot from other central Dublin locations, making it a convenient stop on your city tour.

Phoenix Park

Phoenix Park, one of the largest enclosed public parks in any European capital city, spans over 1,700 acres and serves as a lush, green oasis in Dublin. Established in 1662 as a royal deer park, it remains a sanctuary for wildlife, including a herd of fallow deer that roams freely. The park's vast expanses of grassland, woodlands, and tree-lined avenues make it an ideal location for outdoor activities, family outings, and peaceful retreats from the city's hustle and bustle.

Within Phoenix Park, visitors can explore numerous attractions. The park is home to Áras an Uachtaráin, the official residence of the President of Ireland, which offers guided tours on Saturdays. Dublin Zoo, located within the park, is one of the oldest zoos in the world and a favorite family destination. Other notable sites include the Wellington Monument, the largest obelisk in Europe, and the Papal Cross, erected for Pope John Paul II's visit in 1979. The Victorian People's Flower Gardens and the Phoenix Park Visitor Centre provide additional points of interest for nature enthusiasts and history buffs alike.

When planning your visit to Phoenix Park, consider renting a bike to fully explore its extensive pathways and attractions. The park is open year-round and is free to enter, although some attractions like Dublin Zoo require an admission fee. Picnicking is a popular activity, so bringing along a packed lunch can enhance your experience. Early mornings or late afternoons are ideal times to visit for those seeking tranquility and a chance to see the deer. Make sure to wear comfortable walking shoes and check the park's event calendar for any special activities or guided tours.

Kilmainham Gaol

Kilmainham Gaol, a former prison turned museum, is one of Dublin's most significant historical sites. Opened in 1796 and closed in 1924, the gaol played a crucial role in Irish history, particularly during the struggle for independence. Many leaders of the various uprisings, including the 1916 Easter Rising, were imprisoned and executed here, making it a poignant symbol of Ireland's turbulent past. Today, Kilmainham Gaol serves as a museum and a reminder of the country's fight for freedom.

Visitors to Kilmainham Gaol can take guided tours that provide a detailed account of the prison's history, its notable inmates, and the harsh conditions they endured. The tour includes a visit to the cells, the chapel, and the execution yard, where leaders of the 1916 Easter Rising were executed. The museum exhibits artifacts, photographs, and personal accounts that offer a deeper understanding of the political and social history of the period. The guided tours are informative and often evoke a powerful emotional response, making them an essential part of any visit to Dublin.

To visit Kilmainham Gaol, it's highly recommended to book tickets online in advance, as tours can sell out quickly, especially during peak tourist seasons. The guided tour lasts about an hour, and the site is accessible by public transport, with several bus routes stopping nearby. Wear comfortable shoes, as the tour involves a fair amount of walking. Kilmainham Gaol is not only a must-visit for history enthusiasts but also for anyone seeking to understand Ireland's path to independence and the sacrifices made along the way.

National Museum of Ireland

The National Museum of Ireland, with several branches across Dublin, offers a comprehensive look into the rich history and cultural heritage of Ireland. The museum is divided into three main sites in Dublin: Archaeology, Decorative Arts and History, and Natural History. Each site provides a unique perspective on Ireland's past and present, showcasing everything from ancient artifacts to contemporary design.

The Archaeology branch, located on Kildare Street, is renowned for its extensive collection of artifacts from prehistoric to medieval Ireland. Highlights include the breathtaking Treasury, which houses the Ardagh Chalice, the Tara Brooch, and other exquisite examples of early medieval metalwork. The Kingship and Sacrifice exhibition explores the fascinating world of Iron Age bog bodies, while the Viking Ireland display offers insights into the lives of Ireland's Viking settlers. The Decorative Arts and History branch, located at Collins Barracks, features exhibits on Irish furniture, silver, ceramics, and glass, as well as the history of military service and rebellion in Ireland. The Natural History Museum, affectionately known as the "Dead Zoo," provides an intriguing glimpse into the natural world with its preserved animal specimens.

Admission to all branches of the National Museum of Ireland is free, making it an accessible and budget-friendly activity for visitors. The museums are open year-round, but it's a good idea to check their official website for opening hours and any special exhibitions or events. Guided tours are available and can enhance your understanding of the exhibits. Allocate at least a couple of hours for each site to fully appreciate the collections. Whether you're a history buff, an art lover, or simply curious about Ireland's heritage, the National Museum of Ireland offers an enriching and educational experience.

Dublin's Literary History: James Joyce and Beyond

Dublin's literary heritage is one of the richest in the world, producing an impressive array of writers who have left an indelible mark on literature. At the heart of this legacy is James Joyce, whose works such as "Ulysses" and "Dubliners" are intrinsically linked to the city. Joyce's Dublin is one where every street and building breathes with literary significance, creating a landscape that feels both familiar and profound to those who wander its streets with his works in mind. His writings capture the spirit of Dublin in the early 20th century, painting a vivid picture of its people, their struggles, and their everyday lives.

Beyond Joyce, Dublin has been home to many other literary giants, including Samuel Beckett, W.B. Yeats, Oscar Wilde, and Jonathan Swift. Each of these authors has contributed to the city's reputation as a hub of literary creativity. The influence of these writers is celebrated throughout Dublin, with numerous statues, plaques, and museums dedicated to their memory. The Dublin Writers Museum, located in a beautiful 18th-century mansion on Parnell Square, offers an in-depth look at the lives and works of Ireland's literary legends. Meanwhile, the Irish Writers Centre, also on Parnell Square, continues to foster new talent and provide a space for writers to collaborate and grow.

For literary enthusiasts, there are several must-visit sites in

Dublin. The James Joyce Centre on North Great George's Street provides fascinating exhibits and guided tours related to Joyce's life and works. The annual Bloomsday Festival, held every June 16th, sees fans of Joyce dress in period costume and follow the route taken by Leopold Bloom in "Ulysses." Additionally, Trinity College's Long Room Library not only houses the Book of Kells but also a collection of rare manuscripts and books that are a treasure trove for any book lover. To fully immerse yourself in Dublin's literary culture, consider joining one of the many literary walking tours available, which offer insightful commentary and visits to the city's key literary landmarks.

Final Thoughts

As you wrap up your exploration of Dublin, it's clear that this city offers a unique blend of historical depth, cultural richness, and modern vibrancy. Beyond the well-trodden paths of Trinity College and the Guinness Storehouse, there are countless hidden gems waiting to be discovered. Take the time to explore Dublin's lesser-known attractions, such as the charming Iveagh Gardens or the vibrant street art in the Smithfield and Liberties areas. Engaging with locals, whether in a cozy pub or a bustling market, can provide deeper insights into the city's soul and its enduring charm.

Dublin is a city that rewards the curious traveler. Its compact size makes it easy to explore on foot, allowing you to stumble upon unexpected delights around every corner. Whether it's a quaint bookshop, a historic pub with live traditional music, or a quiet park perfect for reflection, Dublin has a way of making every visitor feel like they've discovered something uniquely their own. For those interested in the arts, Dublin's theatre scene is vibrant and varied, with the historic Abbey Theatre and the modern Bord Gáis Energy Theatre offering performances that range from classic plays to contemporary productions.

To make the most of your time in Dublin, consider purchasing a Dublin Pass, which provides access to many of the city's top attractions and can save you both time and money. Also, remember to dress in layers and carry an umbrella, as Dublin's weather can be unpredictable. Finally, take the opportunity to learn a few Irish phrases; while English is widely spoken, using a bit of the local language can enrich your experience and endear you to the locals. Sláinte!

CHAPTER 2:
The Wild Atlantic Way

The Wild Atlantic Way is one of the world's most spectacular touring routes, stretching over 2,500 kilometers along Ireland's rugged western coast. This breathtaking journey begins in the northern county of Donegal and winds its way south to the vibrant city of Cork. Along the way, travelers are treated to some of the most stunning coastal landscapes, charming villages, and rich cultural heritage that Ireland has to offer. The route is divided into several sections, each with its own unique attractions and experiences, making it an ideal adventure for those looking to explore Ireland's untamed beauty.

This chapter will guide you through the must-see sights and hidden gems of the Wild Atlantic Way, from the towering Cliffs of Moher and the mystical Skellig Michael to the lively streets of Galway and the serene beauty of Connemara National Park. Whether you're an outdoor enthusiast, a history buff, or simply someone seeking the tranquility of nature, the Wild Atlantic Way has something to offer everyone. As you travel along this scenic route, you'll encounter a mix of dramatic landscapes, ancient sites, and warm Irish hospitality that will leave you with unforgettable memories.

When planning your trip, consider renting a car to fully experience the freedom and flexibility of exploring the Wild Atlantic Way at your own pace. Be sure to pack for all weather conditions, as the coastal climate can be unpredictable. Additionally, take advantage of the numerous visitor centers along the route, which provide valuable information on local attractions, accommodations, and activities. With careful planning and an adventurous spirit, the Wild Atlantic Way promises a journey of discovery and wonder.

Cliffs of Moher

The Cliffs of Moher are one of Ireland's most iconic natural landmarks, rising dramatically over 200 meters above the Atlantic Ocean. Located in County Clare, these majestic cliffs stretch for about 8 kilometers along the coast, offering breathtaking views that attract visitors from around the globe. On a clear day, you can see the Aran Islands, Galway Bay, and even the peaks of the Twelve Bens in Connemara from the cliff tops. The sheer scale and beauty of the Cliffs of Moher make them a must-visit destination on the Wild Atlantic Way.

The cliffs are home to a diverse array of wildlife, including numerous seabird species such as puffins, guillemots, and razorbills. The best time to visit for bird watching is during the breeding season from April to July. The Cliffs of Moher Visitor Experience, located at the main viewing area, offers interactive exhibits, informative displays, and a multimedia show that provide insights into the geology, history, and wildlife of the cliffs. Several walking trails along the cliff edge allow visitors to experience the stunning scenery from different vantage points.

For those planning a visit, it's advisable to arrive early in the morning or late in the afternoon to avoid the peak tourist hours. The main visitor center has a car park, and from there, it's a short walk to the cliff edge. Be sure to wear sturdy footwear and bring a jacket, as it can be windy and cool even in the summer months. Guided tours are available for a more in-depth experience, and boat trips from Doolin offer a unique perspective of the cliffs from the sea. Don't forget your camera to capture the awe-inspiring views!

Dingle Peninsula

The Dingle Peninsula, jutting out into the Atlantic Ocean, is a region of extraordinary beauty and rich cultural heritage. Located in County Kerry, this rugged peninsula is renowned for its dramatic landscapes, ancient sites, and vibrant local culture. The scenic drive around the peninsula, known as the Slea Head Drive, offers stunning views of the coastline, distant islands, and rolling green hills dotted with traditional farms and cottages. The town of Dingle, with its colorful buildings and lively pubs, serves as the perfect base for exploring the area. One of the highlights of the Dingle Peninsula is its wealth of archaeological sites, including the Gallarus Oratory, an early Christian church dating back over a thousand years, and the Dunbeg Fort, an ancient promontory fort perched on a cliff edge. The Blasket Islands, visible from the westernmost point of the peninsula, were once home to a thriving Gaelic-speaking community and are now a nature reserve accessible by ferry. The peninsula is also a haven for outdoor activities, offering opportunities for hiking, cycling, and water sports.

When visiting the Dingle Peninsula, take your time to explore the charming town of Dingle, where you can enjoy fresh seafood, traditional music sessions, and a visit to the Dingle Distillery. The Slea Head Drive can be completed in a few hours, but consider spending a full day or more to fully appreciate the sights and experiences. Pack a picnic and enjoy a leisurely stop at one of the many scenic viewpoints along the way. Whether you're exploring ancient ruins, enjoying a pint in a local pub, or simply soaking in the natural beauty, the Dingle Peninsula promises an unforgettable experience.

Ring of Kerry

The Ring of Kerry is one of Ireland's most famous and scenic drives, circling the Iveragh Peninsula in County Kerry. This 179-kilometer route takes you through a landscape of rugged coastlines, majestic mountains, picturesque villages, and historical sites. As you traverse the Ring of Kerry, you'll encounter stunning vistas of the Atlantic Ocean, lush green pastures, and charming seaside towns, making it a highlight of the Wild Atlantic Way. Key attractions along the Ring of Kerry include the Gap of Dunloe, a narrow mountain pass renowned for its breathtaking views, and Muckross House and Gardens, a splendid 19th-century mansion set in Killarney National Park. The Skellig Ring, a scenic detour off the main route, offers views of Skellig Michael, an ancient monastic site perched on a rocky island. The picturesque towns of Kenmare and Sneem provide delightful stops with their colorful shops, traditional pubs, and welcoming atmosphere. Each twist and turn of the road reveals new landscapes, from dramatic cliffs to serene lakes, ensuring that every moment on the Ring of Kerry is filled with wonder.

When planning your journey around the Ring of Kerry, allow a full day to truly appreciate its beauty. Start early to avoid the crowds, especially during the summer months. If you're driving, consider going counterclockwise to make it easier to navigate the narrow roads. There are numerous viewpoints and picnic spots along the route, so pack a lunch and enjoy a leisurely break while taking in the scenery. Be sure to bring a camera to capture the stunning landscapes, and wear comfortable shoes for exploring the many attractions along the way.

Galway City

Galway City, often referred to as Ireland's cultural heart, is a vibrant and lively destination on the west coast. Known for its bohemian atmosphere, bustling arts scene, and rich history, Galway offers a unique blend of old-world charm and contemporary culture. The city's medieval streets are lined with colorful shopfronts, traditional pubs, and an array of cafes and restaurants, creating a dynamic and welcoming environment for visitors.

A stroll through Galway's Latin Quarter is a must, where you can explore the historic Spanish Arch, visit the Galway City Museum, and enjoy street performances by local musicians and artists. Eyre Square, the city's central hub, is a great place to relax and soak up the atmosphere, while the nearby Galway Cathedral offers a peaceful retreat with its stunning architecture and serene interior. The city is also famous for its festivals, including the Galway International Arts Festival and the Galway Races, which draw visitors from around the world.

For those visiting Galway, make sure to indulge in the city's culinary delights, from fresh seafood at McDonagh's to gourmet dishes at Ard Bia at Nimmos. Explore the Claddagh, a historic fishing village just a short walk from the city center, known for its iconic Claddagh ring. Galway's vibrant nightlife is best experienced in its traditional pubs, such as The Crane Bar and Tigh Neachtain, where you can enjoy live Irish music sessions.

With its rich culture and friendly vibe, Galway City promises an unforgettable experience for every traveler.

Connemara National Park

Connemara National Park, located in County Galway, is a stunning expanse of rugged mountains, expansive bogs, heathlands, and woodlands. Covering around 2,957 hectares, the park offers a serene and unspoiled landscape that embodies the wild beauty of Ireland's west coast. Dominated by the Twelve Bens mountain range, Connemara is a paradise for hikers, nature lovers, and those seeking a peaceful retreat into nature.

Visitors to Connemara National Park can explore a variety of walking trails that cater to all levels of fitness and experience. The Diamond Hill trail is particularly popular, offering spectacular views of the surrounding countryside, the Atlantic Ocean, and the nearby islands. The park is also home to an array of wildlife, including Connemara ponies, red deer, and a rich variety of bird species. The visitor center provides informative exhibits on the park's natural and cultural heritage, as well as guided walks and educational programs.

To make the most of your visit to Connemara National Park, wear sturdy hiking boots and bring a waterproof jacket, as the weather can change quickly. The park is open year-round, but the best time to visit is during the spring and summer months when the flora is in full bloom. Pack a picnic to enjoy at one of the scenic spots along the trails, and don't forget your camera to capture the breathtaking landscapes. Whether you're hiking to the summit of Diamond Hill or simply enjoying the tranquility of the park, Connemara offers a profound connection to Ireland's natural beauty.

The Burren

The Burren, located in County Clare, is one of Ireland's most unique and captivating landscapes. This vast karst limestone region, covering approximately 250 square kilometers, is characterized by its stark, moon-like terrain, dotted with ancient stone walls, rare flora, and archaeological sites. The name "Burren" comes from the Irish word "Boireann," meaning "rocky place," which aptly describes this geological wonder. Despite its rugged appearance, the Burren is a place of great beauty and biodiversity, home to over 70% of Ireland's native plant species, including rare Arctic, Mediterranean, and Alpine plants that coexist in this unique environment.

Visitors to the Burren can explore a variety of walking trails that meander through its rocky pavements, offering stunning views and a chance to discover the region's rich history. Among the notable archaeological sites are the Poulnabrone Dolmen, a prehistoric portal tomb dating back to around 3,800 BCE, and the Caherconnell Stone Fort, which provides insights into early Irish settlement. The Burren Perfumery, nestled in the heart of the Burren, offers a delightful experience with its handmade perfumes, cosmetics, and herbal teas inspired by the local flora. To fully appreciate the Burren, consider joining a guided tour with a local expert who can share insights into the geology, ecology, and history of this remarkable region. The Burren National Park offers several well-marked trails suitable for all levels of hikers, with the Carron Loop and the Blackhead Loop being popular choices. The best time to visit is in the spring and early summer when the wildflowers are in bloom. Bring sturdy walking shoes, a camera to capture the unique landscape, and be prepared for changing weather conditions.

Skellig Michael

Skellig Michael, a UNESCO World Heritage site located off the coast of County Kerry, is an extraordinary monastic settlement perched on a rocky island in the Atlantic Ocean. This remote and rugged island, known as "Sceilg Mhichíl" in Irish, was home to a group of ascetic monks who established a monastery here around the 6th century. The island's dramatic landscape, with its steep cliffs and stone steps leading up to the ancient beehive huts, creates a sense of awe and wonder that transports visitors back in time.

The journey to Skellig Michael begins with a boat trip from the mainland, typically departing from Portmagee, Ballinskelligs, or Cahersiveen. The island is renowned for its well-preserved monastic remains, including the beehive cells, oratories, and a medieval church. The site also features a large colony of puffins and other seabirds, making it a haven for birdwatchers. Skellig Michael has gained additional fame in recent years as a filming location for the "Star Wars" saga, adding to its allure for visitors. Due to its remote location and challenging terrain, visiting Skellig Michael requires a good level of fitness and careful planning. Boat trips are weather-dependent and can be canceled at short notice, so it's advisable to have flexible travel plans. Wear sturdy footwear and bring layers to protect against the wind and rain. Guided tours are available and provide valuable insights into the history and significance of the island. Visiting Skellig Michael is a once-in-a-lifetime experience that combines natural beauty, historical intrigue, and a sense of adventure.

Achill Island

Achill Island, the largest of the Irish isles, is situated off the west coast of County Mayo and is known for its dramatic landscapes, pristine beaches, and rich cultural heritage. Connected to the mainland by a bridge, Achill Island offers easy access to visitors who want to explore its rugged beauty and vibrant community. The island is home to some of Ireland's most stunning coastal scenery, including the majestic cliffs of Croaghaun, which are among the highest sea cliffs in Europe, and the picturesque Keem Bay, a secluded beach with crystal-clear waters and white sands.

Achill Island is a paradise for outdoor enthusiasts, offering a range of activities such as hiking, cycling, surfing, and kayaking. The Great Western Greenway, a scenic trail that runs from Westport to Achill, provides a fantastic route for cyclists and walkers to enjoy the island's breathtaking views. The Atlantic Drive, a loop road around the island, offers stunning vistas of the coastline and the surrounding mountains. For history buffs, the Deserted Village at Slievemore is a fascinating site, with the ruins of nearly 100 stone cottages that provide a glimpse into the island's past.

When visiting Achill Island, be sure to explore the island's local arts and crafts scene, with several galleries and workshops showcasing the work of talented artists. The island hosts various festivals throughout the year, including the Achill Seafood Festival and the Achill Island Marathon. For accommodations, you can choose from cozy B&Bs, self-catering cottages, and seaside hotels. The best time to visit is during the summer months when the weather is mild and the days are long. Whether you're seeking adventure, relaxation, or cultural experiences, Achill Island has something to offer every traveler.

Aran Islands

The Aran Islands, located off the coast of County Galway, are a trio of islands that offer a glimpse into traditional Irish life and unspoiled natural beauty. Comprising Inishmore (Inis Mór), Inishmaan (Inis Meáin), and Inisheer (Inis Oírr), the Aran Islands are renowned for their rugged landscapes, ancient stone forts, and strong Gaelic culture. The islands' unique geology, characterized by limestone pavements and cliffs, provides a dramatic backdrop to the vibrant communities that call this place home.

Inishmore, the largest of the three, is famous for Dún Aonghasa, an impressive prehistoric stone fort perched on the edge of a 100-meter-high cliff. The fort, dating back to 1100 BCE, offers breathtaking views of the Atlantic Ocean and is a testament to the islands' rich history. Inishmaan, the middle island, is known for its tranquility and traditional crafts, including the famous Aran sweaters. Inisheer, the smallest island, boasts picturesque landscapes and the ruins of O'Brien's Castle, a 14th-century fortress with stunning views of the surrounding area. Each island has its own distinct charm and offers a unique experience for visitors.

To explore the Aran Islands, consider renting a bike or taking a guided tour to fully appreciate the scenic beauty and historical sites. The islands are accessible by ferry from Doolin or Rossaveal, and during the summer months, flights are available from Connemara Airport. Plan to spend at least a full day on Inishmore to explore its many attractions, while a half-day visit is sufficient for Inishmaan and Inisheer. Bring comfortable walking shoes, a camera, and layers to protect against the unpredictable weather. The Aran Islands offer an unforgettable experience of Ireland's natural and cultural heritage.

Final Thoughts

As you plan your journey along the Wild Atlantic Way, remember that the true essence of travel in Ireland lies in its rich cultural heritage, stunning landscapes, and the warmth of its people. While the popular sites like the Cliffs of Moher and the Ring of Kerry offer spectacular views and memorable experiences, don't overlook the lesser-known gems such as the Burren's unique flora, the mystical allure of Skellig Michael, or the serene beauty of Achill Island. Each destination has its own story to tell, and taking the time to explore these places will enrich your understanding and appreciation of Ireland's diverse regions.

In addition to the main attractions, immerse yourself in local traditions and customs. Attend a traditional music session in a cozy pub, participate in a community festival, or learn a few words of Irish Gaelic to connect with the locals on a deeper level. The Irish are known for their hospitality, and engaging with the community can lead to unexpected friendships and memorable experiences.

While traveling, consider sustainable practices to help preserve the natural beauty and cultural heritage of these areas. Stick to designated trails, support local businesses, and respect the environment. With a spirit of adventure and a sense of respect for the land and its people, your journey through the Wild Atlantic Way will be an unforgettable adventure, leaving you with lasting memories and a deeper connection to the Emerald Isle.

CHAPTER 3:
The Ancient East

The Ancient East of Ireland is a region steeped in history, mythology, and natural beauty. This area, rich with ancient ruins, medieval castles, and verdant landscapes, tells the story of Ireland's past from prehistoric times through the medieval era and beyond. As you journey through the Ancient East, you'll uncover the secrets of early Christian monastic settlements, marvel at the craftsmanship of medieval fortresses, and stand in awe of Neolithic tombs that predate the pyramids of Egypt. This chapter will guide you through some of the most iconic and lesser-known sites in Ireland's Ancient East, offering a glimpse into the country's rich cultural heritage and providing practical tips to enhance your visit.

From the serene valleys of Glendalough to the majestic Rock of Cashel, the Ancient East is a tapestry of historical treasures and scenic landscapes. Each site you visit will transport you back in time, allowing you to walk in the footsteps of saints, scholars, and warriors. As you explore this enchanting region, you'll gain a deeper appreciation for Ireland's storied past and the enduring legacy of its ancient civilizations. Prepare to embark on a journey through history, where every stone and ruin has a tale to tell.

To make the most of your trip, plan your visits to these historic sites in advance, considering the opening hours, guided tour options, and any special events that might be taking place. Wear comfortable walking shoes, as many of these sites involve exploring expansive grounds and uneven terrain. Bring a camera to capture the stunning architecture and landscapes, and consider downloading audio guides or reading up on the history of each site beforehand to enrich your experience. With this chapter as your guide, you'll be well-prepared to uncover the wonders of Ireland's Ancient East.

Glendalough Monastic Site

Glendalough, meaning "Valley of the Two Lakes," is one of Ireland's most significant early Christian monastic sites, founded by St. Kevin in the 6th century. Nestled in the Wicklow Mountains, this picturesque valley is home to a collection of well-preserved ruins, including a round tower, several churches, and a breathtakingly beautiful landscape that has inspired pilgrims and visitors for centuries. The monastic settlement at Glendalough was once a center of learning and spirituality, attracting scholars and monks from all over Europe.

A visit to Glendalough offers the opportunity to explore these ancient ruins while soaking in the natural beauty of the surrounding area. The round tower, standing at 33 meters high, served as a landmark and refuge for monks during Viking raids. St. Kevin's Church, also known as St. Kevin's Kitchen, and the impressive cathedral are among the highlights of the site. The serene lakes and woodland trails provide a perfect setting for reflection and relaxation, making Glendalough a place of both historical and spiritual significance.

To make the most of your visit to Glendalough, start at the Visitor Centre, where you can learn about the site's history and pick up a map of the area. Guided tours are available and highly recommended, as they provide detailed insights into the history and significance of the monastic settlement. Wear sturdy walking shoes and bring weather-appropriate clothing, as the weather in the Wicklow Mountains can be unpredictable. Allow plenty of time to explore the site and take in the natural beauty of the surrounding landscape. Glendalough is open year-round, with the best times to visit being spring and early summer when the area is lush and green.

Kilkenny Castle

Kilkenny Castle, one of Ireland's most iconic medieval fortresses, stands proudly on the banks of the River Nore in the heart of Kilkenny City. Built in 1195 by the Anglo-Norman leader William Marshal, the castle has undergone extensive restorations and is now a major tourist attraction. The castle's grand architecture, beautiful gardens, and rich history make it a must-visit destination for anyone exploring the Ancient East. Kilkenny Castle served as the principal seat of the powerful Butler family for nearly 600 years, and its opulent interiors reflect the wealth and influence of its former inhabitants.

Visitors to Kilkenny Castle can explore its lavishly decorated rooms, including the Long Gallery, with its stunning painted ceiling and collection of portraits, and the Victorian Drawing Room, which offers a glimpse into the elegant lifestyle of the Butler family. The castle grounds are equally impressive, featuring extensive parkland, formal gardens, and a picturesque rose garden. The castle also hosts various exhibitions and events throughout the year, providing an added layer of interest for visitors.

To enhance your visit to Kilkenny Castle, consider taking a guided tour to gain deeper insights into the castle's history and architecture. The castle is open year-round, with extended hours during the summer months. Tickets can be purchased online in advance to avoid queues, especially during peak tourist season. After exploring the castle, take some time to wander around Kilkenny City, known for its medieval streets, vibrant arts scene, and welcoming pubs. The city's rich cultural heritage and lively atmosphere make it a perfect complement to your visit to the castle.

Rock of Cashel

The Rock of Cashel, also known as St. Patrick's Rock, is one of Ireland's most spectacular archaeological sites. Located in County Tipperary, this historic complex sits atop a limestone hill and offers breathtaking views of the surrounding countryside. The site has a rich history dating back to the 5th century when it served as the traditional seat of the kings of Munster. The Rock of Cashel is famous for its impressive collection of medieval buildings, including a round tower, a high cross, a Romanesque chapel, and a Gothic cathedral.

One of the highlights of the Rock of Cashel is the beautifully preserved Cormac's Chapel, which dates back to the 12th century. The chapel is renowned for its intricate stone carvings and well-preserved frescoes, which provide a glimpse into the artistic and religious life of medieval Ireland. The site also includes the Hall of the Vicar's Choral, a 15th-century building that once housed the choir who sang during cathedral services. The Rock of Cashel is a testament to Ireland's rich cultural and religious heritage, making it a must-visit for history enthusiasts and casual tourists alike.

To make the most of your visit to the Rock of Cashel, consider joining a guided tour to gain a deeper understanding of the site's historical significance and architectural features. The visitor center offers informative displays and exhibits, providing context for the monuments you'll explore. The Rock of Cashel is open year-round, with longer opening hours during the summer months. Wear comfortable shoes, as the site involves some uphill walking, and bring a camera to capture the stunning views and architectural details. Nearby, you can also visit the charming town of Cashel, which offers additional dining and accommodation options.

Waterford Crystal Factory

The Waterford Crystal Factory in Waterford City is a world-renowned attraction, offering visitors a fascinating insight into the art of crystal manufacturing. Established in 1783, Waterford Crystal has become synonymous with luxury and craftsmanship, producing some of the finest crystal pieces in the world. The factory tour provides a behind-the-scenes look at the intricate processes involved in creating these exquisite works of art, from glassblowing to cutting and engraving.

During the guided tour, visitors can witness skilled artisans at work, transforming molten glass into beautiful crystal items. The tour includes a visit to the blowing department, where you can see the glassblowers shaping the molten crystal, and the cutting department, where master craftsmen meticulously carve intricate patterns into the glass. The factory also features a showroom displaying a stunning array of finished pieces, from delicate vases and chandeliers to bespoke trophies and glassware. The highlight of the tour is often the opportunity to purchase unique pieces directly from the factory store.

To enhance your visit to the Waterford Crystal Factory, plan to spend at least a couple of hours on the tour and in the showroom. The factory is open year-round, with extended hours during the summer months. It's advisable to book your tour in advance, especially during peak tourist season. Photography is allowed, so bring a camera to capture the craftsmanship in action. After your tour, explore Waterford City's historic Viking Triangle, where you'll find additional attractions, restaurants, and shops.

Newgrange

Newgrange, a prehistoric monument located in County Meath, is one of the most significant archaeological sites in Ireland and a UNESCO World Heritage site. Constructed around 3200 BCE, Newgrange predates Stonehenge and the Great Pyramids of Giza, making it an invaluable treasure of ancient history. This passage tomb is renowned for its massive circular mound, which covers an area of over one acre and is surrounded by 97 large kerbstones, many of which are adorned with intricate carvings. The most remarkable feature of Newgrange is its alignment with the winter solstice. Each year, around December 21st, sunlight enters the tomb's passage and illuminates the inner chamber, creating a spectacular display that has fascinated archaeologists and visitors alike. The site also includes a reconstructed visitor center, where you can learn about the Neolithic people who built Newgrange and the significance of its astronomical alignment. The guided tours provide detailed insights into the construction, history, and mythology surrounding this ancient wonder.

To visit Newgrange, you must book a guided tour through the Brú na Bóinne Visitor Centre, as access to the site is strictly controlled to preserve its integrity. Tours are available year-round, but the winter solstice period is particularly popular, requiring advance booking. Wear comfortable shoes, as the tour involves some walking, and dress in layers to accommodate the cool, damp conditions inside the tomb. Photography is allowed in certain areas, so bring a camera to capture this extraordinary site. Combine your visit with a trip to nearby Knowth and Dowth, other significant prehistoric sites in the Boyne Valley, to gain a comprehensive understanding of Ireland's ancient history.

Hook Lighthouse

Hook Lighthouse, located on the Hook Peninsula in County Wexford, is one of the oldest operational lighthouses in the world, with its origins dating back over 800 years. The lighthouse was built by the Normans in the early 13th century to guide sailors safely into the port of Waterford. Its robust stone structure and iconic black-and-white stripes have made it a landmark on the southeast coast of Ireland. The lighthouse offers stunning views of the rugged coastline and the turbulent waters of the Celtic Sea.

Visitors to Hook Lighthouse can enjoy guided tours that take them up the tower's spiral staircase to the top, where they can marvel at panoramic views of the peninsula and learn about the lighthouse's fascinating history. The tour includes access to the original keepers' quarters, the lantern room, and an exhibition detailing the maritime heritage of the region. The surrounding area is perfect for coastal walks, offering scenic vistas and opportunities to spot marine wildlife, including seals and dolphins.

To make the most of your visit to Hook Lighthouse, plan to spend a few hours exploring the site and its surroundings. The lighthouse is open year-round, with extended hours during the summer months. Be sure to check the weather forecast and dress accordingly, as the coastal winds can be brisk. The visitor center features a café and gift shop, and there are picnic areas where you can relax and enjoy the scenic views. For a more immersive experience, consider timing your visit to coincide with one of the special events or festivals held at the lighthouse throughout the year.

Wicklow Mountains

The Wicklow Mountains, often referred to as the "Garden of Ireland," are a breathtaking expanse of rolling hills, deep valleys, and serene lakes located just south of Dublin. This vast national park encompasses over 20,000 hectares of natural beauty, offering a haven for outdoor enthusiasts and nature lovers. The mountains are home to a variety of flora and fauna, ancient monastic sites, and picturesque villages, making it a diverse and enriching destination.

Hiking is one of the most popular activities in the Wicklow Mountains, with trails ranging from gentle walks to challenging treks. The Wicklow Way, a long-distance trail that stretches over 130 kilometers, traverses the heart of the mountains and offers spectacular views of the surrounding landscapes. Other notable sites include the Powerscourt Waterfall, Ireland's highest waterfall, and Lough Tay, also known as the "Guinness Lake" due to its dark waters and white sandy beach. The area is also rich in history, with ancient ruins like the monastic settlement at Glendalough providing a glimpse into Ireland's past.

When planning a visit to the Wicklow Mountains, allocate a full day or more to fully appreciate the area's natural beauty and historical sites. The park is accessible year-round, but the best time to visit is during the spring and summer months when the weather is mild, and the hills are lush and green. Wear comfortable hiking boots, bring plenty of water and snacks, and don't forget your camera to capture the stunning vistas. Guided tours are available for those who prefer a structured experience, and there are plenty of charming accommodations in nearby villages for an extended stay.

Dunbrody Famine Ship

The Dunbrody Famine Ship, located in New Ross, County Wexford, is a meticulously recreated 19th-century emigrant vessel that offers a poignant and immersive experience of Ireland's Great Famine and subsequent emigration. The original Dunbrody was built in 1845 and carried thousands of Irish emigrants to North America during the famine years. This full-scale replica serves as a living museum, allowing visitors to step back in time and understand the hardships faced by those who left Ireland in search of a better life.

The guided tour of the Dunbrody Famine Ship includes interactive exhibits and costumed performers who bring the history of the ship and its passengers to life. Visitors can explore the cramped steerage quarters where emigrants endured long, perilous journeys across the Atlantic, as well as the more comfortable accommodations of the ship's officers and crew. The experience is both educational and emotional, providing a deep insight into the resilience and determination of the Irish people during one of the most challenging periods in the country's history.

To enhance your visit to the Dunbrody Famine Ship, plan to spend at least a couple of hours exploring the exhibits and taking the guided tour. The visitor center features a café and gift shop, and the adjacent Irish America Hall of Fame honors notable Irish-Americans who have made significant contributions to society. The ship is open year-round, with extended hours during the summer months. New Ross itself is a charming town with additional historical sites and dining options, making it a worthwhile stop on your journey through Ireland's Ancient East.

Boyne Valley

The Boyne Valley, located in County Meath, is a region rich in ancient history and archeological significance, often referred to as the cradle of Irish civilization. It is home to some of Ireland's most iconic prehistoric sites, including Newgrange, Knowth, and Dowth, collectively known as Brú na Bóinne, which are UNESCO World Heritage Sites. These passage tombs date back to around 3200 BCE, making them older than Stonehenge and the Great Pyramids of Giza. Newgrange, in particular, is famous for its winter solstice alignment, where the rising sun illuminates the inner chamber, a phenomenon that draws visitors from around the world.

In addition to its prehistoric monuments, the Boyne Valley is steeped in myth and legend. The Hill of Tara, once the seat of the High Kings of Ireland, is located here and offers panoramic views of the surrounding countryside. Tara is also associated with many ancient Irish legends, including tales of the Tuatha Dé Danann and the legendary Lia Fáil, or Stone of Destiny. Nearby, the Battle of the Boyne Visitor Centre commemorates the pivotal 1690 battle between King William III and King James II, a turning point in Irish and British history.

To fully appreciate the Boyne Valley's rich heritage, plan to spend at least a full day exploring its sites. The visitor centers at Newgrange and the Battle of the Boyne provide excellent starting points, offering guided tours and interpretative exhibits that bring the history of the area to life. Wear comfortable walking shoes, as the terrain can be uneven, and bring a camera to capture the stunning landscapes and ancient structures. The Boyne Valley is easily accessible from Dublin, making it a convenient and enriching day trip.

Final Thoughts

As you embark on your journey through Ireland's Ancient East, remember that the magic of this region lies not only in its well-known landmarks but also in its hidden gems and the stories of its people. While the major sites like Newgrange and the Rock of Cashel offer incredible insights into Ireland's past, don't overlook the smaller, lesser-known attractions that provide a more intimate glimpse into the country's rich cultural tapestry. Take the time to explore local markets, engage with the community, and perhaps even partake in a traditional music session at a local pub. When planning your visit, consider the seasonal variations in Ireland's weather. The summer months provide longer days and generally milder weather, making it an ideal time for outdoor exploration. However, the off-peak seasons can offer a more tranquil experience with fewer crowds and the opportunity to see the landscape in a different light. Regardless of when you visit, packing layers and waterproof gear is advisable to stay comfortable in Ireland's often unpredictable climate.

Lastly, embrace the spirit of adventure and curiosity that defines travel in Ireland. Each region has its own unique charm and character, waiting to be discovered. Whether you're delving into ancient history, enjoying the vibrant arts and culture, or simply soaking in the stunning natural beauty, Ireland's Ancient East promises an unforgettable experience. As you journey through this captivating part of the world, let the stories, traditions, and landscapes of Ireland leave an indelible mark on your heart. Safe travels!

CHAPTER 4:
Northern Ireland

Northern Ireland, with its dramatic landscapes and deep historical roots, is a region that offers a unique blend of natural beauty and rich cultural heritage. From the rugged coastlines and mystic geological formations to the vibrant cities steeped in history, Northern Ireland invites you to explore and uncover its many treasures. The area is known for its breathtaking scenery, including the famous Giant's Causeway and the Mourne Mountains, as well as significant cultural landmarks like Titanic Belfast and the historic Derry City Walls. Each location tells a story, reflecting the resilience and spirit of its people.

In this chapter, we will journey through some of Northern Ireland's most iconic sites, offering insights and practical tips to help you make the most of your visit. Whether you are traversing the legendary Giant's Causeway, delving into the maritime history at Titanic Belfast, or walking the ancient city walls of Derry, you will find that Northern Ireland is a place of profound contrasts and captivating stories. Prepare to be enchanted by the wild beauty and historical depth that this region has to offer.

From adrenaline-pumping adventures at the Carrick-a-Rede Rope Bridge to the tranquil elegance of Mount Stewart, Northern Ireland caters to every type of traveler. As you embark on this exploration, remember to immerse yourself in the local culture, savor the traditional cuisine, and engage with the friendly locals. This guide aims to provide you with not only the must-see attractions but also the hidden gems that make Northern Ireland a truly unique and unforgettable destination.

Giant's Causeway

The Giant's Causeway, a UNESCO World Heritage Site, is one of Northern Ireland's most spectacular natural wonders. Located on the north coast in County Antrim, this iconic site features around 40,000 interlocking basalt columns, the result of an ancient volcanic eruption. The columns, mostly hexagonal, create a surreal and captivating landscape that has inspired myths and legends for centuries. According to local folklore, the causeway was built by the giant Fionn mac Cumhaill (Finn MacCool) as a bridge to Scotland.

A visit to the Giant's Causeway begins at the award-winning visitor center, where you can learn about the geological and mythological history of the site through interactive exhibits and audiovisual displays. From there, follow the well-marked trails that lead down to the causeway itself. The main path is accessible and offers stunning views of the columns and the surrounding coastline. For the more adventurous, the cliff-top trail provides a more challenging hike with panoramic views of the area.

When planning your trip to the Giant's Causeway, allocate a few hours to fully explore the site. The best time to visit is during the early morning or late afternoon to avoid the crowds and capture the best light for photography. Wear sturdy shoes, as the rocks can be slippery, and bring a windproof jacket, as the coastal weather can be unpredictable. The visitor center has a café and gift shop, and guided tours are available for those who want a more in-depth understanding of the site's history and geology.

Titanic Belfast

Titanic Belfast, located in the heart of Belfast's Titanic Quarter, is a world-class museum dedicated to the story of the RMS Titanic. Opened in 2012, the centenary year of the ship's launch, this state-of-the-art attraction is housed in an iconic building whose design reflects the ship's bow. The museum's nine interactive galleries tell the story of the Titanic from its conception and construction in Belfast's Harland and Wolff shipyard to its tragic maiden voyage and enduring legacy.

Visitors to Titanic Belfast can explore the shipyard, walk through a full-scale replica of the Titanic's hull, and experience the ship's luxurious interiors through innovative displays and re-creations. Highlights include the Shipyard Ride, which takes you through the shipbuilding process, and the Ocean Exploration Centre, where you can learn about the discovery of the Titanic wreck and ongoing underwater exploration. The museum also features personal stories of the passengers and crew, providing a poignant and human perspective on the disaster.

To make the most of your visit to Titanic Belfast, plan to spend at least a few hours exploring the exhibits. Tickets can be booked online in advance, and it's advisable to visit during off-peak hours to avoid crowds. The museum is open year-round, with extended hours during the summer. There are several dining options within the complex, including the Bistro 401 and the Galley Café, offering a range of meals and refreshments. Don't forget to visit the Titanic Store for unique souvenirs and gifts related to Belfast's maritime heritage.

Carrick-a-Rede Rope Bridge

The Carrick-a-Rede Rope Bridge, located near Ballintoy in County Antrim, is one of Northern Ireland's most thrilling attractions. Originally constructed by salmon fishermen over 350 years ago, the bridge spans 20 meters and is suspended 30 meters above the rocky coastline, connecting the mainland to the tiny island of Carrick-a-Rede. The crossing offers stunning views of Rathlin Island and even Scotland on a clear day, making it a must-visit for adventure seekers and nature lovers alike.

The surrounding area, managed by the National Trust, features beautiful coastal paths that provide spectacular views of the rugged coastline and the vibrant blue waters of the North Atlantic. The walk to the bridge is part of the experience, with well-maintained trails that guide visitors through some of Northern Ireland's most dramatic scenery. Along the way, you might spot a variety of seabirds, including puffins and guillemots, adding to the site's natural allure.

When planning your visit to Carrick-a-Rede, aim to arrive early in the day to avoid the crowds, especially during the peak tourist season. The bridge is open year-round, but weather conditions can affect accessibility, so it's wise to check ahead. Wear sturdy footwear for the walk to the bridge, and if you're crossing, be prepared for the exhilarating (and slightly nerve-wracking) experience. The nearby village of Ballintoy offers several quaint cafés and pubs where you can relax and enjoy local cuisine after your adventure.

Dark Hedges

The Dark Hedges, located near Ballymoney in County Antrim, is a captivating avenue of beech trees that has become one of Northern Ireland's most photographed locations. Planted in the 18th century by the Stuart family to impress visitors approaching their Georgian mansion, Gracehill House, the trees have grown over the years to form an eerie, atmospheric tunnel. This natural archway has gained international fame as a filming location for the HBO series "Game of Thrones," where it portrayed the Kingsroad.

The haunting beauty of the Dark Hedges makes it a popular spot for photographers and tourists alike. The best time to visit is either early in the morning or late in the afternoon when the light filtering through the branches creates a magical effect. In the autumn, the leaves turn vibrant shades of orange and red, adding to the avenue's mystique. Although it's a public road, traffic is minimal, allowing visitors to stroll along the lane and capture stunning images without too much disturbance.

To make the most of your visit to the Dark Hedges, consider combining it with a trip to nearby attractions such as the Giant's Causeway and Carrick-a-Rede Rope Bridge. Parking is available at the Hedges Hotel, a short walk from the site. While there are no entry fees, it's important to respect the natural environment by not climbing the trees or damaging the area. Local guides offer walking tours that provide historical context and interesting anecdotes about this iconic location.

Derry City Walls

The Derry City Walls, encircling the old city of Derry (also known as Londonderry), are among the best-preserved city walls in Europe and a significant symbol of Northern Ireland's turbulent history. Built between 1613 and 1619 by the Honourable The Irish Society as defenses for early 17th-century settlers from England and Scotland, the walls stretch for approximately 1.5 kilometers and are complete with gates, bastions, and cannons. They offer a fascinating walk with panoramic views of the city and its surroundings.

Walking the walls provides a unique perspective on Derry's past, from the Siege of Derry in 1689 to the more recent Troubles. The walls encompass several key historical sites, including St. Columb's Cathedral, the Guildhall, and the Apprentice Boys Memorial Hall. Informative plaques and guided tours are available to help visitors understand the significance of the landmarks and events associated with the walls. The Peace Bridge, connecting the city to the Ebrington Square, is also visible from the walk and symbolizes the city's ongoing journey towards peace and reconciliation.

To fully appreciate the Derry City Walls, start your visit at the Tower Museum or the Siege Museum, both of which offer comprehensive exhibits on the city's history. The best times to walk the walls are in the morning or late afternoon when the light is ideal for photography. Wear comfortable shoes for the walk, which can take around an hour at a leisurely pace. After exploring the walls, spend some time in Derry's vibrant city center, enjoying its rich cultural offerings and friendly atmosphere.

Mount Stewart

Mount Stewart, located in County Down, is one of Northern Ireland's most enchanting estates. This 19th-century mansion, surrounded by world-renowned gardens, offers a glimpse into the opulent lifestyle of the aristocratic Londonderry family. The house itself is a treasure trove of art and antiques, with beautifully preserved rooms that reflect the grandeur and elegance of the period. Highlights include the Italian Drawing Room, with its exquisite décor, and the Central Hall, featuring a stunning domed ceiling.

The gardens at Mount Stewart are the real star, having earned international acclaim for their beauty and diversity. Designed by Edith, Lady Londonderry, the gardens are divided into several themed areas, each with its unique character and charm. The Italian Garden, the Spanish Garden, and the Dodo Terrace are particularly noteworthy, offering vibrant displays of flowers, topiary, and statuary. The estate also features woodland walks and a picturesque lake, providing a tranquil retreat for visitors.

When visiting Mount Stewart, plan to spend several hours exploring both the house and gardens. The estate is open year-round, with different seasonal highlights in the gardens. Guided tours of the house are available and highly recommended to gain a deeper understanding of its history and the family who lived there. The onsite café offers a selection of refreshments, and there is a gift shop where you can purchase souvenirs and local crafts. Comfortable walking shoes are advisable for the extensive garden trails.

The Mourne Mountains

The Mourne Mountains, located in County Down, are a stunning range of granite peaks that offer some of the best hiking and outdoor experiences in Northern Ireland. These mountains, which inspired C.S. Lewis's magical land of Narnia, are characterized by their dramatic landscapes, with sweeping views, rocky outcrops, and tranquil valleys. The highest peak, Slieve Donard, stands at 850 meters and provides a challenging yet rewarding climb with panoramic views stretching to the Isle of Man and Scotland on clear days.

The Mournes are not only for experienced hikers; they offer trails suitable for all levels of fitness and adventure. The Mourne Wall Walk is particularly popular, tracing an 18-mile route along a historic dry-stone wall that traverses 15 summits. For a more leisurely experience, the Tollymore Forest Park, located at the foothills of the Mournes, offers scenic walks through ancient woodland, along rivers, and past stunning viewpoints.

When planning your visit to the Mourne Mountains, ensure you have appropriate gear for hiking, including sturdy boots, layered clothing, and a map. The weather can be unpredictable, so it's best to be prepared for changing conditions. The nearby towns of Newcastle and Warrenpoint offer accommodation and dining options, making them excellent bases for exploring the mountains. Guided tours are available for those who prefer a more structured experience or want to learn more about the region's natural and cultural history.

Bushmills Distillery

The Old Bushmills Distillery, located in the village of Bushmills in County Antrim, is the world's oldest licensed whiskey distillery, having been granted a license to distill in 1608. This historic distillery is renowned for its smooth and flavorful Irish whiskeys, which are crafted using traditional methods passed down through generations. Visitors to the distillery can take guided tours to learn about the whiskey-making process, from mashing and fermentation to distillation and aging.

The tour of Bushmills Distillery is a sensory journey, allowing guests to see, smell, and taste the whiskey at various stages of production. Highlights include the copper pot stills, the oak aging casks, and the bottling hall. At the end of the tour, visitors are treated to a tasting session where they can sample some of Bushmills' finest whiskeys, including the signature Bushmills Original, the rich and complex Black Bush, and the exclusive Bushmills 21 Year Old Single Malt.

To make the most of your visit to Bushmills Distillery, book your tour in advance, especially during peak tourist seasons. The distillery is open year-round, and tours typically last about an hour. The onsite shop offers a wide range of Bushmills products, including limited edition whiskeys that are not available elsewhere. The distillery also features a cozy café where you can enjoy a meal or a snack before or after your tour. Combining your visit with a trip to the nearby Giant's Causeway can make for a perfect day out in County Antrim.

Castle Ward

Castle Ward, located near Strangford in County Down, is a striking 18th-century mansion set on a beautiful 820-acre walled demesne. Known for its unique blend of architectural styles, Castle Ward showcases both classical and Gothic designs, reflecting the differing tastes of its original owners, Lord Bangor and his wife, Lady Ann Bligh. The estate's grandeur is evident in its lavishly decorated rooms, including the elegant dining room, the richly adorned library, and the grand staircase hall.

Beyond the mansion, Castle Ward offers extensive grounds with a mix of gardens, woodlands, and trails that are perfect for leisurely walks and exploring nature. The Victorian sunken garden, the Temple Water, and the woodland trails provide picturesque settings for a day outdoors. The estate is also famous for its connection to the popular TV series "Game of Thrones," where it served as the filming location for Winterfell. Visitors can take guided tours to learn about the estate's history and its role in the iconic series.

When planning your visit to Castle Ward, allocate a full day to explore both the house and the grounds. The estate is open year-round, with different events and activities depending on the season. The on-site tea room offers a delightful selection of refreshments, and the gift shop features local crafts and souvenirs. For those interested in "Game of Thrones," specialized tours and archery experiences are available. Comfortable footwear is recommended for walking the extensive grounds, and don't forget to bring a camera to capture the stunning scenery.

Final Thoughts

Exploring Northern Ireland offers a journey through a land steeped in history, natural beauty, and rich cultural traditions. From the iconic landscapes of the Giant's Causeway and the Mourne Mountains to the historical depths of Derry's city walls and the vibrant culture of Belfast, each location provides a unique glimpse into the region's heritage and charm. While this guide covers many notable sites, Northern Ireland is full of hidden gems and local experiences waiting to be discovered. When planning your trip, consider incorporating lesser-known attractions and activities that allow you to connect with the local community. Attend a traditional music session in a cozy pub, explore the local food markets, or participate in community events to gain a deeper understanding of Northern Ireland's vibrant culture. Engaging with locals can offer invaluable insights and enhance your travel experience.

For a comprehensive and fulfilling visit, balance your itinerary with a mix of well-known landmarks and off-the-beaten-path adventures. This approach not only diversifies your experience but also supports sustainable tourism by spreading the economic benefits across different areas. Remember to respect the natural environment and cultural heritage sites, ensuring that future generations can enjoy them as well.

In summary, Northern Ireland is a destination that captivates with its dramatic landscapes, historical richness, and warm hospitality. Whether you're an adventurer, a history buff, or simply looking to relax and soak in the scenery, Northern Ireland has something to offer everyone. Embrace the spirit of exploration, and let the magic of this beautiful region unfold before you.

CHAPTER 5: IRELAND'S HIDDEN GEMS   73

CHAPTER 5:
Ireland's Hidden Gems

Ireland is famed for its well-trodden tourist paths, but beyond the popular destinations lie hidden gems that offer equally breathtaking experiences without the crowds. These lesser-known spots, from secluded parks to untouched landscapes, provide a more intimate glimpse into Ireland's natural beauty and cultural heritage. Exploring these hidden gems allows travelers to connect deeply with the essence of the Emerald Isle, discovering tranquil environments and unique stories that add a special touch to their journey. Among Ireland's hidden treasures are national parks, charming villages, and ancient sites that hold the key to the country's rich history and natural wonders. These locations often remain under the radar, offering solitude and a sense of adventure. Whether it's hiking through rugged terrains, uncovering historical ruins, or simply enjoying the serene landscapes, these hidden gems promise memorable experiences away from the hustle and bustle of more popular tourist spots.

To make the most of your trip, venture off the beaten path and explore these lesser-known destinations. Equip yourself with good maps and a spirit of curiosity, and you will find that Ireland's hidden gems reveal the heart and soul of this enchanting island. These places not only showcase the diverse beauty of Ireland but also offer a tranquil escape where you can fully immerse yourself in the landscape and culture.

Burren National Park

Burren National Park, located in County Clare, is a unique landscape characterized by its extensive limestone pavements, interspersed with patches of grassland, hazel scrub, and woodland. This starkly beautiful area, often described as a moonscape, is home to a rich diversity of flora and fauna, making it a paradise for botanists and nature enthusiasts. The park covers approximately 1,500 hectares and is part of the larger Burren region, renowned for its archaeological sites and vibrant cultural heritage.

The Burren's distinctive landscape was formed over millions of years by glacial activity and erosion, resulting in its trademark limestone terraces and crevices. Visitors can explore several marked trails that wind through the park, offering stunning views and the chance to observe rare plant species such as orchids, gentians, and ferns. The park also provides a habitat for a variety of wildlife, including pine martens, foxes, and a plethora of bird species.

For those planning to visit Burren National Park, it's best to go between April and September when the flora is at its most vibrant. The park has several well-maintained walking trails, ranging from easy strolls to more challenging hikes. It's advisable to wear sturdy footwear and bring a camera to capture the breathtaking scenery. The Burren Visitor Centre in nearby Kilfenora provides maps, guides, and information about the park's geology, ecology, and history, ensuring a well-rounded and informative visit.

Glenveagh National Park

Glenveagh National Park, located in County Donegal, is one of Ireland's most remote and beautiful national parks. Covering over 16,000 hectares of rugged mountains, pristine lakes, and lush woodlands, Glenveagh offers a serene escape into nature. At its heart lies Glenveagh Castle, a stunning 19th-century mansion surrounded by exquisitely maintained gardens. The park is a haven for hikers, wildlife enthusiasts, and those seeking tranquility in a breathtaking setting.

The park's dramatic landscapes are dominated by the Derryveagh Mountains, with Mount Errigal being the highest peak. Hiking trails of varying difficulty levels crisscross the park, providing opportunities for both leisurely walks and challenging climbs. The park is also home to a herd of red deer and a sanctuary for golden eagles, making it a prime spot for wildlife watching. The picturesque Lough Veagh adds to the park's scenic charm, offering peaceful lakeside walks and picnic spots.

Visitors to Glenveagh National Park should allocate at least a day to explore its many attractions. The visitor center near the main entrance offers informative exhibits and guided tours of the castle and gardens. It's recommended to wear suitable hiking gear and bring a picnic to enjoy by the lake or in the gardens. For those interested in extended hikes, the Glenveagh Mountain Trail provides a rewarding challenge with panoramic views of the park's rugged beauty. The park is open year-round, but the best time to visit is during the warmer months when the gardens are in full bloom and the weather is ideal for outdoor activities.

Slieve League Cliffs

The Slieve League Cliffs, located in County Donegal, are among the highest sea cliffs in Europe, reaching a staggering height of nearly 2,000 feet (600 meters) above the Atlantic Ocean. These cliffs offer some of the most dramatic coastal views in Ireland, with sheer drops and rugged landscapes that captivate visitors. Unlike the more famous Cliffs of Moher, Slieve League provides a more secluded and tranquil experience, allowing visitors to fully appreciate the raw beauty of Ireland's coastline without the crowds.

The cliffs are part of the Slieve League Peninsula, a region rich in history and natural beauty. Walking trails lead up to various viewpoints, offering breathtaking panoramas of the Atlantic Ocean and the surrounding countryside. The most popular route is the Pilgrim's Path, which takes you from the Bunglas viewpoint to the top of the cliffs, providing stunning vistas along the way. The area is also steeped in mythology and folklore, adding an element of mystery and intrigue to your visit.

To fully enjoy the Slieve League Cliffs, plan your visit on a clear day to take advantage of the spectacular views. Wear sturdy hiking boots and bring a windproof jacket, as the weather can be unpredictable. There are no entrance fees, and the car park at Bunglas is free, making it an affordable day out. Consider stopping by the Slieve League Cliffs Centre before your hike for maps and information on guided tours. The centre also has a café where you can enjoy a warm drink and a bite to eat after your hike.

Valentia Island

Valentia Island, located off the southwest coast of County Kerry, is a hidden gem known for its rich history, stunning landscapes, and outdoor activities. Accessible by a bridge from the mainland or by ferry, this small island offers a unique blend of natural beauty and cultural heritage. It is one of Ireland's westernmost points, providing dramatic coastal views and a sense of tranquility that is perfect for those looking to escape the hustle and bustle of daily life.

The island is home to several notable attractions, including the Skellig Experience Visitor Centre, which provides insights into the nearby Skellig Islands, a UNESCO World Heritage Site. Visitors can explore the island's lush gardens, scenic walking trails, and historic sites such as the Knightstown Lighthouse and the 6th-century monastic settlement at Church Island. Valentia Island is also renowned for its fossilized tetrapod tracks, which date back 385 million years, making it a significant site for geology enthusiasts.

When visiting Valentia Island, take time to explore its scenic walking trails, such as the Bray Head Loop, which offers panoramic views of the Atlantic Ocean and the Skellig Islands. The island is also a great spot for water sports, including kayaking, snorkeling, and diving. Be sure to visit during the summer months when the weather is mild and the ferry services are frequent. The island has several accommodation options, from cozy bed and breakfasts to self-catering cottages, ensuring a comfortable stay for all visitors.

Beara Peninsula

The Beara Peninsula, stretching between County Cork and County Kerry, is one of Ireland's most unspoiled and picturesque regions. Known for its rugged coastline, lush landscapes, and charming villages, the peninsula offers a perfect retreat for nature lovers and those seeking a peaceful escape. The Beara Way, a long-distance walking route, encircles the peninsula, providing an immersive way to explore its diverse scenery, from rolling hills and tranquil lakes to dramatic sea cliffs.

The peninsula is dotted with quaint villages such as Allihies, Castletownbere, and Eyeries, each offering a unique glimpse into the local culture and way of life. Visitors can explore historical sites, including ancient stone circles, ring forts, and the ruins of Dunboy Castle. The area is also home to Dursey Island, accessible by Ireland's only cable car, which offers stunning views and a chance to experience the island's rich flora and fauna.

To make the most of your visit to the Beara Peninsula, plan to spend several days exploring its many attractions and natural beauty spots. The Beara Way is ideal for hiking enthusiasts, offering various sections that cater to different fitness levels. Don't miss the opportunity to take the cable car to Dursey Island for an unforgettable adventure. Local accommodations range from cozy guesthouses to charming inns, providing a comfortable base for your explorations. The best time to visit is during the late spring and summer months when the weather is favorable for outdoor activities.

Doolough Valley

Doolough Valley, located in County Mayo, is one of Ireland's most hauntingly beautiful landscapes, known for its dramatic scenery and historical significance. This remote valley, flanked by the Mweelrea and Sheeffry Hills, offers a sense of tranquility and isolation, making it a perfect destination for those seeking solace in nature. The valley is characterized by its deep, glacial lake, rugged terrain, and sweeping views, providing a stark and stunning backdrop for outdoor enthusiasts.

The valley is also steeped in history, marked by a tragic event known as the Doolough Tragedy. In 1849, during the Great Famine, hundreds of destitute people were forced to walk from Louisburgh to Delphi Lodge in search of relief. Many perished along the way, and today, a memorial cross stands in the valley to honor their memory. This historical context adds a poignant dimension to the natural beauty of Doolough Valley, making it a place of reflection as well as recreation.

Visitors to Doolough Valley can enjoy a variety of activities, including hiking, photography, and picnicking by the lake. The valley is accessible by car, with scenic drives offering breathtaking views at every turn. For those interested in hiking, the Delphi Mountain Resort offers guided walks that explore the surrounding hills and valleys. Be sure to bring sturdy footwear, as the terrain can be challenging. The best time to visit is during the spring and summer months when the weather is mild and the landscape is at its most vibrant.

Inishbofin Island

Inishbofin Island, located off the coast of County Galway, is a hidden gem that offers a glimpse into traditional Irish island life. Known for its unspoiled landscapes, vibrant wildlife, and rich cultural heritage, Inishbofin is an ideal destination for nature lovers and those seeking a tranquil escape. The island is accessible by ferry from Cleggan and offers a peaceful retreat from the mainland's hustle and bustle.

The island's name, which means "Island of the White Cow" in Irish, reflects its ancient myths and legends. Inishbofin is home to several historical sites, including the ruins of Cromwell's Barracks and St. Colman's Abbey. The island also boasts beautiful sandy beaches, scenic walking trails, and a variety of habitats that support a wide range of bird species, making it a haven for birdwatchers. The Marine Research Station on the island provides further insights into the local marine life and conservation efforts.

To make the most of your visit to Inishbofin, plan to spend at least a couple of days exploring its natural and cultural attractions. Accommodation options range from charming bed and breakfasts to cozy guesthouses, ensuring a comfortable stay. The island is perfect for walking and cycling, with several well-marked trails that showcase its diverse landscapes. Don't miss the chance to enjoy traditional music sessions at the local pubs, where you can experience the island's vibrant cultural scene firsthand. The best time to visit is during the summer months when the weather is warm and the island's flora and fauna are in full bloom.

Kylemore Abbey

Kylemore Abbey, located in the heart of Connemara in County Galway, is one of Ireland's most iconic and picturesque attractions. This stunning Gothic Revival castle, set against the backdrop of the Twelve Bens mountains and overlooking a serene lake, is a must-visit destination for anyone exploring the west of Ireland. Originally built as a private residence in the 19th century, Kylemore Abbey has a rich history and is now home to a community of Benedictine nuns.

The abbey's beautiful Victorian walled garden, chapel, and tranquil woodland walks make it a place of peace and reflection. The gardens, restored to their former glory, showcase a wide variety of plants and flowers, offering a delightful experience for horticulture enthusiasts. The Gothic chapel, often referred to as a "cathedral in miniature," is an architectural gem with intricate carvings and stained glass windows that reflect the craftsmanship of the era. Visitors to Kylemore Abbey can enjoy guided tours that provide insights into its history, architecture, and the daily life of the nuns who live there. The on-site café offers a range of delicious homemade treats, and the gift shop features products made by the nuns, including chocolates and skincare items. To make the most of your visit, plan to spend a few hours exploring the grounds and soaking in the serene atmosphere. The abbey is open year-round, but the gardens are at their most beautiful in the spring and summer months.

Lough Gur

Lough Gur, situated in County Limerick, is a place of profound historical and archaeological significance, offering a window into Ireland's ancient past. This horseshoe-shaped lake, surrounded by lush green hills and dotted with prehistoric sites, is one of Ireland's most important archaeological landscapes. The area has been inhabited for over 6,000 years, with evidence of Neolithic settlements, Bronze Age tombs, and medieval structures, making it a treasure trove for history enthusiasts.

Visitors to Lough Gur can explore various ancient sites, including stone circles, wedge tombs, and the remains of an early Christian church. The Grange Stone Circle, Ireland's largest stone circle, is particularly notable and provides a glimpse into the spiritual and communal lives of Ireland's early inhabitants. The site is also home to the remains of crannogs, ancient man-made islands that served as fortified dwellings during the Iron Age and early medieval period. The rich archaeological tapestry of Lough Gur offers a fascinating journey through time, highlighting the enduring human presence in this tranquil landscape.

To fully appreciate Lough Gur, a visit to the Lough Gur Heritage Centre is highly recommended. The centre provides detailed exhibits on the area's history, including interactive displays and artifacts unearthed from local excavations. Guided tours are available, offering in-depth insights into the significance of the various sites around the lake. For those looking to explore the natural beauty of Lough Gur, several walking trails offer scenic routes around the lake, providing opportunities for birdwatching and photography. The area is open year-round, but the best time to visit is during the spring and summer months when the weather is pleasant, and the surrounding landscape is in full bloom.

Final Thoughts

Visiting Ireland's hidden gems offers an unparalleled opportunity to delve into the country's rich tapestry of history, culture, and natural beauty. While the more famous landmarks certainly warrant a visit, these lesser-known sites provide a deeper, more intimate connection to Ireland's heritage and landscapes. Each location, from the haunting beauty of Doolough Valley to the serene elegance of Kylemore Abbey, tells a unique story and offers a distinctive experience that enriches any travel itinerary. When planning your visit to these hidden gems, it's essential to consider the practical aspects to make your journey smooth and enjoyable. Ensure you have reliable transportation, as many of these sites are off the beaten path and not always accessible by public transport. Renting a car can provide the flexibility needed to explore these remote areas at your own pace. Additionally, take advantage of local knowledge by engaging with guides and visiting heritage centres, which can enhance your understanding and appreciation of each site.

While these destinations offer a retreat from the more crowded tourist spots, they also embody the essence of Ireland's charm and hospitality. Take the time to immerse yourself fully in the experiences they offer, whether it's a reflective walk through ancient ruins, a peaceful hike along dramatic cliffs, or a leisurely exploration of a historic island. Each of these hidden gems adds a unique layer to your Irish adventure, ensuring that your journey through this enchanting country is both memorable and transformative.

IRELAND TRAVEL GUIDE

CHAPTER 6:
Coastal and Countryside Retreats

· · · · · · · · · · · · · ·

Ireland's coastline and countryside offer some of the most breathtaking and serene landscapes in the world. From dramatic cliffs and pristine beaches to rolling hills and tranquil lakes, these areas provide a perfect escape from the hustle and bustle of city life. This chapter explores the beauty and charm of Ireland's coastal and countryside retreats, highlighting places where nature's splendor is on full display. Whether you're seeking a peaceful getaway, outdoor adventures, or a deep connection with nature, Ireland's coastal and countryside areas have something to offer every traveler.

Exploring these retreats allows you to experience the authentic Irish way of life, where traditions are preserved, and the pace of life is slower. You can stroll through quaint villages, visit ancient castles, and enjoy the hospitality of the local people. Activities such as hiking, cycling, fishing, and wildlife watching are abundant, providing opportunities to immerse yourself in the natural beauty and tranquility of the Irish landscape.

As you plan your journey through Ireland's coastal and countryside retreats, be prepared for a mix of weather conditions. Layered clothing, waterproof gear, and sturdy walking shoes are essential. Renting a car can enhance your experience, allowing you to explore remote areas at your own pace. Engage with locals, respect the environment, and savor the simplicity and beauty of Ireland's countryside.

Bantry Bay and the Sheep's Head Peninsula

Bantry Bay, located in County Cork, is a stunning inlet stretching from the Atlantic Ocean into the heart of West Cork. Known for its serene waters and picturesque surroundings, Bantry Bay offers a tranquil retreat with a rich history and vibrant local culture. The area is dotted with charming villages, historical sites, and lush gardens. Bantry House, a stately home with beautiful gardens overlooking the bay, is a must-visit. The house, dating back to the 18th century, offers a glimpse into Ireland's aristocratic past and provides stunning views of the bay.

Adjacent to Bantry Bay is the Sheep's Head Peninsula, a narrow strip of land jutting out into the Atlantic. This peninsula is a hiker's paradise, renowned for the Sheep's Head Way, a network of trails offering panoramic views of the coastline, mountains, and countryside. The trails vary in difficulty, catering to both casual walkers and seasoned hikers. The Sheep's Head Lighthouse, located at the tip of the peninsula, is a popular spot offering breathtaking views of the rugged coastline.

For those visiting Bantry Bay and the Sheep's Head Peninsula, consider staying in a local B&B or guesthouse to experience genuine Irish hospitality. Enjoy fresh seafood at local restaurants, explore the trails, and visit the weekly Bantry market for local crafts and produce. The area is ideal for outdoor enthusiasts and those looking to unwind in a serene setting. Remember to pack comfortable walking shoes, a rain jacket, and a camera to capture the stunning landscapes.

Kinsale:
Gourmet Capital

Kinsale, often referred to as the gourmet capital of Ireland, is a picturesque coastal town in County Cork. Famous for its culinary delights, Kinsale is home to a plethora of restaurants, cafes, and pubs offering a diverse array of gastronomic experiences. The town's culinary reputation is celebrated annually during the Kinsale Gourmet Festival, attracting food enthusiasts from all over the world. From fresh seafood and traditional Irish dishes to international cuisine, Kinsale's vibrant food scene caters to all tastes.

Beyond its culinary fame, Kinsale boasts a rich maritime history and charming streets lined with colorful buildings. Charles Fort, a star-shaped fortress dating back to the late 17th century, is a significant historical landmark offering spectacular views of Kinsale Harbour. The town is also known for its lively arts scene, with numerous galleries, craft shops, and festivals showcasing local talent. Walking tours of Kinsale provide insights into its history, culture, and architecture.

When visiting Kinsale, make dining a central part of your itinerary. Book a table at one of the acclaimed restaurants like Fishy Fishy or The Black Pig Winebar. Explore the town's historical sites, enjoy a boat trip on the harbor, and take a leisurely stroll through the winding streets. For a unique experience, participate in a cooking class or food tour to learn about local ingredients and cooking techniques. Kinsale's welcoming atmosphere and culinary excellence make it a must-visit destination on Ireland's south coast.

Donegal's Wild Coast

Donegal's Wild Coast, part of Ireland's Wild Atlantic Way, is renowned for its untamed beauty, dramatic landscapes, and rich cultural heritage. This region, located in the northwest of Ireland, boasts rugged cliffs, pristine beaches, and vast stretches of unspoiled countryside. Donegal's coastline is characterized by its wild, windswept nature, offering breathtaking views and a sense of solitude that is hard to find elsewhere. Visitors to this area can explore the stunning Slieve League Cliffs, which are among the highest sea cliffs in Europe, offering spectacular vistas over the Atlantic Ocean.

The region is also home to several charming villages and towns, each with its unique character and attractions. The town of Donegal itself is a hub of cultural and historical significance, featuring Donegal Castle and the ancient Abbey of Donegal. Additionally, the coastal town of Bundoran is known for its vibrant surf culture, attracting surfers from around the globe to its impressive waves. Whether you're hiking the coastal trails, exploring historical sites, or simply relaxing on a secluded beach, Donegal's Wild Coast offers a wealth of experiences for nature lovers and adventurers alike.

When visiting Donegal's Wild Coast, be sure to pack appropriately for the variable weather conditions, including waterproof clothing and sturdy walking boots. Consider renting a car to explore the region at your own pace, allowing you to visit off-the-beaten-path locations and enjoy the stunning scenery. Local accommodations, ranging from cozy bed and breakfasts to charming coastal cottages, provide a warm welcome and an authentic Irish experience. Don't miss the opportunity to sample local seafood and traditional Irish dishes at the many pubs and restaurants scattered throughout the region.

Westport and Clew Bay

Westport, located in County Mayo, is a picturesque town known for its Georgian architecture, lively atmosphere, and stunning natural surroundings. Nestled at the edge of Clew Bay, Westport is a gateway to a myriad of outdoor adventures and cultural experiences. The town itself is characterized by its tree-lined streets, colorful buildings, and friendly locals. Westport House, a grand estate with beautifully landscaped gardens and a rich history, is a major attraction, offering guided tours and a variety of family-friendly activities.

Clew Bay, with its 365 islands, provides a breathtaking backdrop for a range of water-based activities. Kayaking, sailing, and fishing are popular pursuits, allowing visitors to explore the bay's unique landscape and abundant wildlife. The Great Western Greenway, a scenic cycling and walking trail that stretches from Westport to Achill Island, is a must-do for outdoor enthusiasts, offering panoramic views of the bay and surrounding countryside. Westport is also known for its vibrant arts scene, with numerous galleries, music venues, and festivals celebrating local culture and talent.

For those visiting Westport and Clew Bay, consider staying in one of the town's charming accommodations, from boutique hotels to cozy guesthouses. Renting a bicycle or joining a guided tour can enhance your exploration of the area, providing insights into its history and natural beauty. Be sure to visit the local markets and artisan shops to purchase unique souvenirs and support local craftspeople. Dining in Westport is a delight, with a wide range of restaurants offering fresh seafood, traditional Irish dishes, and international cuisine.

Baltimore and the Islands

Baltimore, a charming village in County Cork, serves as the perfect base for exploring the islands of Roaringwater Bay and beyond. Known for its picturesque harbor, vibrant maritime culture, and rich history, Baltimore is a haven for sailors, seafood lovers, and anyone seeking a tranquil retreat by the sea. The village's waterfront is dotted with colorful boats, and the local pubs and restaurants are renowned for their fresh seafood, particularly the famous Baltimore prawns.

The nearby islands, including Sherkin Island, Cape Clear Island, and Heir Island, offer a wealth of opportunities for exploration and adventure. Sherkin Island, just a short ferry ride from Baltimore, is known for its beautiful beaches, walking trails, and the ruins of a Franciscan abbey. Cape Clear Island, Ireland's southernmost inhabited island, is a Gaeltacht area where visitors can experience traditional Irish culture, language, and hospitality. The island is also a hotspot for birdwatching, with its bird observatory attracting enthusiasts from around the world. When planning a visit to Baltimore and the surrounding islands, consider staying in one of the village's charming bed and breakfasts or guesthouses for an authentic Irish experience. Take advantage of the regular ferry services to explore the islands, and be sure to pack comfortable walking shoes, a camera, and binoculars for birdwatching. Enjoy the local seafood and traditional Irish music sessions at the village's pubs, and immerse yourself in the unique maritime culture and natural beauty of this idyllic corner of Ireland.

Kenmare and the Beara Peninsula

Kenmare, nestled in County Kerry, is a picturesque town known for its charming streets, vibrant arts scene, and stunning natural surroundings. This welcoming town is a gateway to the Beara Peninsula, a rugged and scenic region offering some of Ireland's most breathtaking landscapes. Kenmare itself boasts a rich history, evident in its well-preserved Georgian architecture and historical landmarks such as the Kenmare Stone Circle. The town is also famous for its excellent dining options, with numerous restaurants offering delicious local cuisine.

The Beara Peninsula, located to the southwest of Kenmare, is a haven for outdoor enthusiasts and those seeking tranquility. This area is characterized by its dramatic coastal cliffs, rolling hills, and ancient sites. One of the highlights is the Beara Way, a long-distance walking trail that loops around the peninsula, providing spectacular views and access to remote villages and historical ruins. The Healy Pass, a winding mountain road, offers breathtaking vistas and is a must-drive for visitors exploring the region by car.

When visiting Kenmare and the Beara Peninsula, consider staying in one of the many charming bed and breakfasts or boutique hotels that offer warm Irish hospitality. Take time to explore the local shops, galleries, and craft stores in Kenmare, and enjoy a meal at one of the town's renowned restaurants. For those looking to experience the Beara Peninsula's natural beauty, hiking the Beara Way or driving the Healy Pass are highly recommended. Don't forget to pack comfortable walking shoes and a camera to capture the stunning scenery.

Bundoran: Surfing Hotspot

Bundoran, located in County Donegal, is known as Ireland's surfing capital and attracts wave enthusiasts from around the globe. This vibrant seaside town offers some of the best surfing conditions in the country, thanks to its Atlantic swells and diverse range of surf breaks. The town's main beach, Tullan Strand, is particularly popular among surfers of all skill levels, offering consistent waves and a beautiful backdrop of sand dunes and cliffs. Bundoran is also home to several surf schools and rental shops, making it easy for beginners to get started.

In addition to its surfing scene, Bundoran boasts a lively atmosphere with plenty of activities and attractions for visitors. The town features a variety of entertainment options, including amusement parks, live music venues, and a bustling nightlife. Bundoran's coastal location also makes it an ideal spot for other water sports such as kayaking, paddleboarding, and sea fishing. For those who prefer to stay on land, there are numerous scenic walking and cycling routes that offer stunning views of the coastline and countryside.

When planning a trip to Bundoran, consider booking a stay at one of the many accommodations ranging from cozy guesthouses to modern hotels. Surf lessons and equipment rentals are widely available, with several reputable surf schools offering group and private lessons. Don't miss the chance to explore the town's other attractions, such as the Bundoran Adventure Park and Waterworld, an indoor aqua park. For dining, Bundoran offers a range of options from casual beachside cafes to fine dining restaurants, ensuring a variety of culinary experiences.

Lough Erne in Fermanagh

Lough Erne, located in County Fermanagh, is a stunning lake district known for its tranquil beauty and rich history. This area, consisting of two connected lakes, Upper and Lower Lough Erne, offers a serene escape with numerous opportunities for outdoor activities and exploration. The lakes are dotted with over 150 islands, many of which are home to ancient ruins, monastic sites, and unique wildlife. One of the most notable islands is Devenish Island, which features a well-preserved monastic site dating back to the 6th century.

The Lough Erne region is ideal for water-based activities such as boating, fishing, and kayaking. The calm waters and picturesque surroundings make it a perfect destination for a leisurely boat trip or a peaceful day of fishing. For those who enjoy walking and cycling, the area offers several scenic trails, including the popular Cuilcagh Boardwalk Trail, also known as the Stairway to Heaven, which provides breathtaking views from the summit of Cuilcagh Mountain. The Marble Arch Caves Global Geopark is another must-visit attraction, offering guided tours of the stunning limestone caves and surrounding landscape.

Visitors to Lough Erne can choose from a variety of accommodations, including lakeside lodges, cozy bed and breakfasts, and luxurious hotels. Renting a boat or booking a guided tour is a great way to explore the lakes and their islands. Be sure to visit the local markets and shops to purchase unique crafts and local produce. For dining, the region offers several excellent restaurants and cafes, many of which focus on locally sourced ingredients and traditional Irish cuisine.

Killary Harbour: Ireland's Fjord

Killary Harbour, located on the border between Counties Galway and Mayo, is Ireland's only fjord and one of the country's most spectacular natural attractions. This nine-mile-long inlet is surrounded by dramatic mountains, including the Mweelrea Mountains, which are the highest in Connacht. The fjord's unique landscape of steep cliffs, rugged terrain, and deep waters provides a stunning backdrop for outdoor activities and exploration. Whether you're interested in hiking, boating, or simply soaking in the natural beauty, Killary Harbour offers an unforgettable experience.

The area around Killary Harbour is rich in history and culture, with numerous archaeological sites and traditional Irish villages to explore. The nearby village of Leenane, known as the "Gateway to Connemara," is a charming spot with quaint shops, pubs, and accommodation options. The fjord itself is a haven for marine life, including dolphins, seals, and a variety of seabirds, making it a great destination for wildlife enthusiasts. Boat tours of the fjord are available, providing visitors with the opportunity to learn about the area's geology, history, and ecology from knowledgeable guides.

For those looking to explore the region, several hiking trails offer breathtaking views of Killary Harbour and the surrounding landscape. The Killary Harbour Coastal Walk is a popular route that takes hikers along the southern shore of the fjord, providing stunning vistas and access to secluded beaches. Another notable trail is the Famine Walk, which follows the path taken by local residents during the Great Famine in the 1840s. This historic route offers a poignant reminder of the region's past while showcasing its natural beauty.

Final Thoughts

Ireland, with its rich history, vibrant culture, and stunning land-scapes, offers an unparalleled travel experience. From the bus-tling streets of Dublin to the serene beauty of the Wild Atlantic Way and the ancient sites of the Ancient East, this guide has explored the diverse regions that make Ireland a unique and captivating destination. Each chapter has provided insights into the must-see attractions, hidden gems, and cultural experiences that await visitors, ensuring that your journey through Ireland is both enriching and memorable.

As you prepare for your trip, consider the practical tips and advice offered throughout this guide. Whether you're navigat-ing the winding roads of the countryside, exploring the lively cities, or immersing yourself in the local culture, being well-pre-pared will enhance your experience and help you make the most of your time in Ireland. Remember to respect the natural envi-ronment, support local businesses, and engage with the friendly and welcoming Irish people, who are an integral part of what makes this country so special.

In addition to the well-known attractions, take the time to dis-cover some of Ireland's lesser-known treasures. Visit the small villages, enjoy the traditional music sessions in local pubs, and explore the scenic walking trails that reveal the true essence of the Irish landscape. Whether you're an adventure seeker, a his-tory buff, or simply looking to relax and unwind, Ireland has something to offer every traveler. Embrace the spirit of explo-ration and let the magic of Ireland inspire and captivate you on your journey.

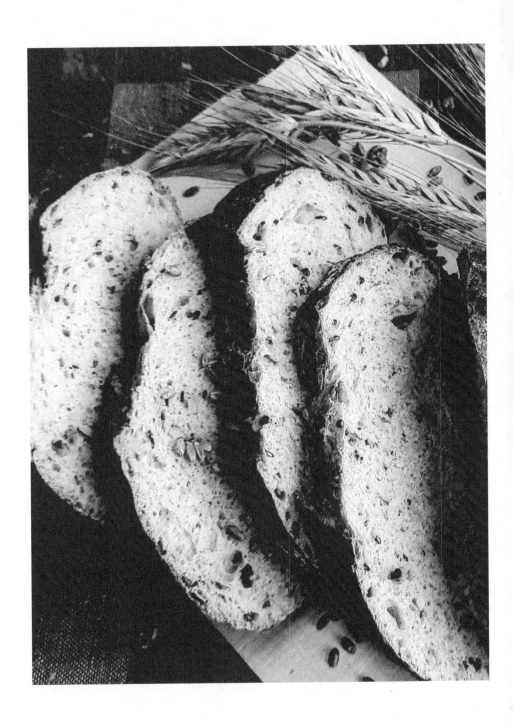

CHAPTER 7:
Irish Cuisine

· · · · · · · · · · · · · · · · · · · ·

Irish cuisine is a delightful journey into the heart of the Emerald Isle, reflecting its rich history, vibrant culture, and abundant natural resources. The culinary landscape of Ireland has evolved significantly over the years, blending traditional recipes with modern influences to create a diverse and flavorful food scene. From hearty breakfasts to fresh seafood and innovative dining experiences, Irish cuisine offers something for every palate. This chapter delves into the culinary delights of Ireland, exploring its signature dishes, regional specialties, and the best places to enjoy these gastronomic treats.

The foundation of Irish cuisine is built on simple, high-quality ingredients sourced from the country's lush landscapes and bountiful seas. Traditional dishes often feature potatoes, meat, and dairy products, reflecting Ireland's agricultural heritage. However, in recent years, the country's food scene has embraced global influences, resulting in a fusion of old and new that appeals to both locals and visitors alike. Whether you're enjoying a comforting bowl of Irish stew or sampling contemporary creations in a Michelin-starred restaurant, Irish cuisine is sure to leave a lasting impression.

To fully appreciate Ireland's culinary offerings, it's essential to explore both its traditional fare and its modern innovations. This chapter will guide you through the essential elements of

Irish cuisine, from the iconic full Irish breakfast to the freshest seafood and everything in between. We'll also provide practical tips on where to dine, what to try, and how to make the most of your culinary adventure in Ireland.

Traditional Irish Breakfast

The traditional Irish breakfast is a beloved culinary institution, providing a hearty start to the day that reflects the country's agricultural roots. This substantial meal typically includes a variety of items such as bacon, sausages, black and white pudding, eggs, baked beans, grilled tomatoes, and mushrooms, all served with slices of toast or soda bread. In many places, you may also find additional components like potato farls or boxty, adding a regional twist to the classic breakfast spread.

The origins of the full Irish breakfast can be traced back to the early 19th century, when it was commonly enjoyed by farmers before heading out for a long day of work. Today, it remains a popular choice for both locals and tourists, offering a comforting and filling meal that showcases the best of Irish produce. The combination of savory flavors and hearty textures makes it a perfect way to start your day, whether you're exploring the countryside or the bustling streets of Dublin.

For the best traditional Irish breakfast experience, seek out local cafes and guesthouses that take pride in using fresh, locally sourced ingredients. Popular spots include The Woollen Mills in Dublin, where you can enjoy a full Irish breakfast with a modern twist, or The Lemon Tree in Kenmare, known for its authentic and delicious offerings. Wherever you choose to dine, be sure to savor every bite and enjoy the warm hospitality that accompanies this iconic meal.

Seafood Delicacies:
Oysters, Mussels, and More

Ireland's coastal waters are teeming with fresh seafood, making it a paradise for seafood lovers. From succulent oysters and plump mussels to tender crab and flavorful fish, the country's seafood delicacies are a true highlight of its culinary landscape. Irish seafood is celebrated for its quality and freshness, often caught and served on the same day, ensuring a taste experience that is both vibrant and satisfying.

Oysters are a particular favorite in Ireland, with Galway Bay oysters being among the most famous. These briny delights are typically enjoyed raw, often with a squeeze of lemon or a dash of hot sauce. Mussels are another popular choice, commonly steamed with garlic, white wine, and herbs, creating a fragrant and mouthwatering dish. Crab, lobster, and various fish such as salmon and cod also feature prominently on Irish menus, each prepared with care to highlight their natural flavors.

To enjoy the best of Irish seafood, visit coastal towns and seafood festivals where you can sample a wide variety of dishes. The Galway International Oyster Festival is a must-visit event for oyster enthusiasts, offering a chance to taste the finest oysters and enjoy live music and entertainment. For a more intimate dining experience, head to restaurants like Moran's Oyster Cottage in Galway or Fishy Fishy in Kinsale, where you can savor freshly prepared seafood in a charming setting. Don't forget to pair your meal with a pint of Guinness or a glass of crisp white wine to complete the experience.

Irish Stew and Coddle

Irish stew and coddle are two of Ireland's most cherished comfort foods, embodying the heart and soul of Irish culinary tradition. Irish stew, typically made with lamb or mutton, potatoes, carrots, onions, and sometimes parsnips, is a hearty dish that has warmed the bellies of the Irish for generations. The simplicity of the ingredients, slow-cooked to perfection, allows the flavors to meld into a rich and satisfying meal. This dish is not only a staple in Irish homes but also a highlight in many traditional pubs and restaurants across the country.

Coddle, a Dublin specialty, is another classic dish that tells the story of Ireland's resourcefulness and culinary ingenuity. Traditionally made with sausages, bacon, potatoes, and onions, all simmered in a broth, coddle was historically a way to use up leftovers. Its comforting and savory flavors make it a popular choice during the colder months. Both Irish stew and coddle are emblematic of the Irish approach to food – using simple, high-quality ingredients to create meals that are both nourishing and delicious.

To experience these traditional dishes at their best, visit renowned establishments such as The Brazen Head in Dublin, which claims to be Ireland's oldest pub, serving hearty Irish stew, or The Hairy Lemon, known for its authentic coddle. For those wanting to try their hand at making these dishes, many cooking schools offer classes where you can learn the secrets to perfecting these Irish classics. Additionally, attending local food festivals, like the Dublin Bay Prawn Festival, can provide opportunities to taste a variety of traditional Irish dishes.

Farm-to-Table Experiences

Ireland's commitment to sustainable agriculture and fresh, locally sourced ingredients is showcased in its burgeoning farm-to-table dining scene. This movement emphasizes the connection between the land, the farmer, and the diner, ensuring that the food served is as fresh and flavorful as possible. Farm-to-table restaurants often feature seasonal menus that highlight the best produce, meat, and dairy from local farms, creating a dining experience that is both environmentally responsible and delicious.

One of the leading figures in this movement is Ballymaloe House and Cookery School in County Cork, which has long championed the use of local, organic ingredients. Here, guests can enjoy meals prepared with produce from the estate's own gardens and farm. Another notable destination is The Brook-Lodge & Macreddin Village in County Wicklow, which houses The Strawberry Tree, Ireland's first certified organic restaurant. Dining at such establishments not only supports local farmers and sustainable practices but also offers an authentic taste of Ireland's rich agricultural heritage.

For those interested in exploring Ireland's farm-to-table offerings, consider visiting farmers' markets, such as the English Market in Cork or St. George's Market in Belfast. These markets provide an opportunity to meet local producers and sample fresh, artisanal products. Additionally, many farms offer tours and workshops, allowing visitors to see firsthand where their food comes from and to gain a deeper appreciation for Ireland's agricultural traditions.

Artisan Cheeses and Local Delicacies

Ireland's lush pastures and favorable climate make it an ideal place for dairy farming, and the country is renowned for its high-quality cheeses and dairy products. Artisan cheesemakers across Ireland produce a wide variety of cheeses, from creamy blues and robust cheddars to unique creations that incorporate local herbs and flavors. Some of the most famous Irish cheeses include Cashel Blue, a rich and tangy blue cheese from County Tipperary, and Durrus, a semi-soft cheese with a distinctive flavor from West Cork.

In addition to cheese, Ireland boasts a range of other local delicacies that are well worth seeking out. Black and white pudding, made from pork, oatmeal, and spices, are traditional components of the full Irish breakfast but are also enjoyed on their own or as part of other dishes. Irish soda bread, with its characteristic crumbly texture and slightly tangy flavor, is another staple that perfectly complements hearty soups and stews.

To discover the best of Irish cheeses and local delicacies, visit specialty shops and markets, such as Sheridan's Cheesemongers, which has locations throughout Ireland and offers an impressive selection of Irish and international cheeses. Food festivals, like the Listowel Food Fair and the Dingle Food Festival, are also fantastic venues to sample a wide variety of local products and meet the artisans behind them. Whether enjoyed as part of a meal or on their own, these Irish delicacies provide a delicious taste of the country's culinary heritage.

Bakeries and Sweet Treats

Ireland's bakery scene is a delightful blend of traditional recipes and contemporary flavors, offering a range of sweet treats that are sure to satisfy any palate. From the rich, buttery scones and soda bread to the delectable pastries and cakes, Irish bakeries are known for their warm, homey atmosphere and delicious offerings. Traditional Irish scones, often served with clotted cream and jam, are a must-try and can be found in nearly every bakery across the country. Irish soda bread, made with baking soda instead of yeast, is another staple that pairs perfectly with soups and stews.

In addition to these classics, many Irish bakeries have embraced international influences, creating unique twists on traditional recipes. You'll find bakeries offering everything from French-inspired pastries to American-style cookies and cakes. Some standout bakeries include The Bretzel Bakery in Dublin, known for its artisanal breads and pastries, and The Tiller + Grain, which offers a modern take on traditional Irish baking. These establishments not only showcase the diversity of Irish baking but also highlight the quality of local ingredients used in their creations.

For a truly indulgent experience, visit one of Ireland's many cafes and patisseries that specialize in sweet treats. Places like Queen of Tarts in Dublin and Griffins Bakery in Galway are renowned for their delicious cakes, tarts, and pastries. Whether you're looking for a classic apple tart or a decadent chocolate cake, these bakeries offer a wide array of options that will satisfy your sweet tooth. Be sure to visit local farmers' markets as well, where you can find homemade jams, jellies, and other sweet delights to take home.

Pubs and Gastropubs

Ireland's pub culture is legendary, and no visit to the country would be complete without experiencing its vibrant and welcoming pub scene. Traditional pubs are the heart of social life in Ireland, offering a cozy atmosphere where locals and visitors alike can enjoy a pint of Guinness, live music, and hearty pub fare. Irish pubs are known for their character and charm, often featuring dark wood interiors, roaring fireplaces, and friendly patrons. Popular dishes include fish and chips, shepherd's pie, and bangers and mash, all of which pair perfectly with a cold pint of beer.

In recent years, gastropubs have emerged as a popular dining option, combining the casual atmosphere of a pub with high-quality, innovative cuisine. These establishments focus on using fresh, local ingredients to create dishes that are both flavorful and beautifully presented. Some well-known gastropubs include The Exchequer in Dublin, which offers a modern twist on traditional Irish dishes, and O'Connell's in Galway, known for its gourmet burgers and craft beers. Gastropubs provide a unique dining experience that highlights the best of Irish culinary creativity and hospitality.

For those looking to experience the best of Irish pub culture, be sure to visit iconic establishments such as The Temple Bar in Dublin, known for its lively atmosphere and extensive whiskey collection, and The Crown Liquor Saloon in Belfast, renowned for its Victorian-era decor and historic significance. Many pubs also feature live music sessions, offering an authentic taste of traditional Irish music and dance. To make the most of your pub experience, consider joining a pub crawl or guided tour, which can provide insights into the history and culture of these beloved institutions.

Fine Dining
and Michelin-Starred Restaurants

Ireland's culinary landscape has seen a significant transformation in recent years, with a growing number of fine dining establishments and Michelin-starred restaurants making their mark. These venues offer exceptional dining experiences, showcasing the talents of some of the country's most acclaimed chefs. Fine dining in Ireland emphasizes the use of high-quality, locally sourced ingredients, often highlighting the best of Irish produce, meat, and seafood. The result is a menu that is both innovative and deeply rooted in the country's culinary traditions.

Some of Ireland's top fine dining destinations include Chapter One in Dublin, which has earned a Michelin star for its contemporary Irish cuisine, and The Cliff House Hotel in Ardmore, known for its stunning seaside views and exquisite dishes. These restaurants offer tasting menus that change with the seasons, ensuring that each visit provides a unique and memorable experience. The emphasis on creativity and presentation, combined with impeccable service, makes fine dining in Ireland a true gastronomic delight.

For those seeking a Michelin-starred experience, Ireland boasts several renowned restaurants that have been recognized for their excellence. Patrick Guilbaud in Dublin, which holds two Michelin stars, is famed for its elegant French-inspired cuisine, while Aniar in Galway focuses on a farm-to-table approach, offering dishes that celebrate the region's natural bounty. Dining at these establishments is an opportunity to indulge in some of the finest cuisine Ireland has to offer, making it a highlight of any culinary journey through the country.

Food Festivals and Farmers' Markets

Ireland's food festivals and farmers' markets are vibrant celebrations of the country's rich culinary heritage and local produce. These events offer a platform for local farmers, artisans, and chefs to showcase their best products, from fresh vegetables and meats to handmade cheeses and baked goods. Festivals such as the Galway International Oyster and Seafood Festival, held annually in September, highlight Ireland's seafood bounty with tastings, cooking demonstrations, and lively competitions. The Dingle Food Festival is renowned for its bustling market and cookery demonstrations, attracting food enthusiasts from around the world.

Farmers' markets are a staple of Irish communities, providing fresh, locally-sourced food and a taste of regional specialties. Markets like the English Market in Cork, which has been operating since 1788, offer a variety of stalls selling everything from artisanal breads and cheeses to fresh fish and meat. Dublin's Temple Bar Food Market is another favorite, known for its organic produce and gourmet street food. These markets not only support local farmers and producers but also offer visitors a chance to sample authentic Irish flavors and ingredients.

To fully experience Ireland's food festivals and farmers' markets, plan your visit around these events. Check local listings for market days and festival dates, and arrive early to explore the full range of offerings. Don't hesitate to chat with the vendors—they're often eager to share the stories behind their products and offer cooking tips. Bring a reusable bag to carry your purchases and be prepared to sample a little bit of everything. These culinary gatherings provide a delightful and delicious way to immerse yourself in Irish culture.

Final Thoughts

As you prepare to embark on your journey through Ireland, remember that the true essence of this beautiful country lies not only in its scenic landscapes and historic landmarks but also in its vibrant culture and warm, welcoming people. Beyond the well-trodden paths and iconic sights, Ireland offers countless hidden gems waiting to be discovered. Take the time to explore the lesser-known areas, engage with locals, and immerse yourself in the traditions and stories that make Ireland unique.

Whether you're wandering through ancient monastic sites, hiking along rugged coastal cliffs, or savoring a hearty Irish stew in a cozy pub, each experience will add a layer of depth to your adventure. Respect the local customs and environment, support local businesses, and embrace the spirit of adventure that Ireland inspires. As you navigate through the diverse regions of this enchanting land, may your journey be filled with unforgettable moments, new friendships, and a deeper appreciation for the rich tapestry of Irish life.

Ireland's charm lies in its ability to surprise and delight at every turn. From the bustling streets of Dublin to the tranquil beauty of the countryside, each chapter of this guide is designed to help you make the most of your visit. Keep an open mind, a sense of curiosity, and a willingness to step off the beaten path. Here's to your Irish adventure—may it be as magical and memorable as the land itself. Sláinte!

CHAPTER 8:
Traveling in Ireland, Practical Tips

Traveling through Ireland offers an enchanting mix of historic landmarks, vibrant cities, and breathtaking natural landscapes. From the bustling streets of Dublin to the serene beauty of the Wild Atlantic Way, Ireland caters to every type of traveler. This chapter aims to provide practical tips to make your journey smooth and enjoyable, covering the best times to visit, accommodation options, transportation, and other essential travel advice. Whether you are a solo traveler, a couple, or a family, these tips will help you navigate Ireland with ease, ensuring that you make the most of your visit to this captivating country.

Choosing the Right Time to Visit

Ireland's weather can be quite unpredictable, but each season offers its unique charm. The best time to visit largely depends on what you want to experience. Spring (March to May) and autumn (September to November) are ideal for avoiding the peak tourist season while still enjoying mild weather and fewer crowds. During these times, the countryside blooms with flowers in spring, and autumn brings a vibrant display of colors.

Summer (June to August) is the most popular time to visit, offering longer days and warmer temperatures, making it perfect for outdoor activities and festivals. However, it is also the busiest and most expensive time of year. Winter (December to February) can be cold and wet, but it is a magical time to explore Ireland's festive Christmas markets, cozy pubs, and stunning winter landscapes.

When planning your trip, consider the specific activities you want to enjoy. For example, hiking and outdoor adventures are best in the summer, while cultural experiences and city tours can be enjoyed year-round. Always pack layers and waterproof gear, as Ireland's weather can change quickly.

Accommodation

Ireland offers a wide range of accommodation options to suit every budget and preference. For budget travelers, hostels and budget hotels provide affordable lodging with basic amenities. Popular hostel chains like Generator and Kinlay Hostel are well-rated and conveniently located in major cities like Dublin and Galway. Budget hotels and bed and breakfasts (B&Bs) are also plentiful, offering comfortable rooms and often a hearty Irish breakfast.

For those seeking mid-range options, there are numerous boutique hotels and guesthouses that offer a charming and personalized stay. These accommodations often feature unique decor, locally sourced breakfasts, and a warm, welcoming atmosphere. Examples include The Dean in Dublin and The Twelve Hotel in Galway.

Luxury travelers can indulge in Ireland's top-tier hotels and castles, which offer opulent rooms, fine dining, and exceptional service. Ashford Castle in County Mayo and The Merrion Hotel in Dublin are renowned for their luxurious amenities and historical significance. Many of these luxury accommodations also offer spa services, golf courses, and other exclusive experiences.

When booking accommodation, consider the location and proximity to the attractions you wish to visit. Staying in central areas can save travel time and provide easier access to dining and entertainment options. Booking in advance, especially during peak seasons, ensures better availability and rates.

Transportation

Navigating Ireland can be a delightful part of your journey, with various transportation options to suit different travel styles and preferences. Renting a car is one of the most popular choices for travelers who want the freedom to explore at their own pace. Ireland's well-maintained road network allows you to reach even the most remote and picturesque locations. When renting a car, keep in mind that driving is on the left side of the road, and some rural roads can be quite narrow. It's also worth considering renting a smaller vehicle for easier maneuvering through tight spaces and finding parking in city centers.

Public transportation is another viable option, especially for those who prefer not to drive. Ireland's public transit system includes trains, buses, and trams, connecting major cities and towns efficiently. Irish Rail offers scenic train routes that allow you to relax and enjoy the landscape while traveling between destinations such as Dublin, Galway, and Cork. Bus Eireann provides extensive bus services covering both urban and rural areas, making it easy to visit smaller towns and attractions. In

Dublin, the Luas tram system is an efficient way to navigate the city's key areas.

For more flexible and localized travel, consider using rideshare services like Uber or local taxi companies. Biking is also a popular option, especially in bike-friendly cities like Dublin, which has a public bike-sharing scheme called DublinBikes. Additionally, many towns and cities are very walkable, allowing you to explore at a leisurely pace. When planning your transportation, consider combining different modes to make the most of your time and convenience.

Traveling on a Budget

Ireland can be an affordable destination if you plan wisely and take advantage of budget-friendly options. Start by booking flights and accommodation well in advance to secure the best deals. Use comparison websites to find the cheapest flights, and consider traveling during the off-peak season (spring and autumn) when prices for flights and accommodation are generally lower. Staying in hostels, budget hotels, or Airbnb accommodations can significantly reduce your lodging costs, and many hostels offer private rooms if you prefer more privacy.

Eating out can add up quickly, so take advantage of local markets, grocery stores, and budget-friendly eateries. Try traditional Irish dishes at pubs, which often offer hearty meals at reasonable prices. Street food and food trucks are also great for sampling local cuisine without breaking the bank. Additionally, many attractions, such as museums and galleries, have free admission days or reduced prices for students and seniors. Exploring Ireland's natural beauty, including national parks, beaches, and scenic trails, is usually free and offers some of the most memorable experiences.

Utilizing public transportation instead of renting a car can also help keep costs down. Look for transportation passes, such as the Leap Card in Dublin, which offers discounted fares on buses, trains, and trams. Many cities also have walking tours that are either free or operate on a pay-what-you-want basis. Planning your activities and budgeting accordingly will allow you to enjoy all that Ireland has to offer without overspending.

Health and Safety Tips

Staying healthy and safe during your trip to Ireland involves a few key considerations. Firstly, ensure you have travel insurance that covers medical expenses, as healthcare in Ireland can be expensive for non-residents. Ireland's healthcare system is generally of high quality, with numerous pharmacies and clinics available. It's wise to carry a basic first-aid kit and any necessary medications, as some areas, especially rural ones, may have limited access to medical facilities.

Safety-wise, Ireland is considered a very safe destination, with low crime rates. However, it's still important to take standard precautions. Keep an eye on your belongings, especially in crowded tourist areas and public transportation. Avoid walking alone in unfamiliar areas at night, and always use well-lit, populated routes. Be mindful of the weather, which can be unpredictable. Carrying waterproof clothing and sturdy footwear will help you stay comfortable and safe during outdoor activities.

For emergency situations, familiarize yourself with local emergency numbers: 999 or 112 for police, fire, and medical emergencies. It's also helpful to know the location of your country's embassy or consulate in Ireland. By staying prepared and aware, you can ensure a safe and enjoyable trip to this beautiful country.

Internet and Connectivity

Staying connected in Ireland is generally straightforward, with widespread access to reliable internet and mobile networks. Major cities like Dublin, Galway, and Cork have extensive Wi-Fi coverage, including free Wi-Fi in public spaces such as libraries, cafes, and shopping centers. Hotels, hostels, and many B&Bs also offer free Wi-Fi, though the quality and speed can vary, especially in more rural areas. For those needing consistent and high-speed connectivity, coworking spaces and business centers are readily available in urban areas, providing excellent facilities for remote work.

Mobile connectivity is robust across Ireland, with several providers offering prepaid SIM cards that can be easily purchased upon arrival. Companies like Vodafone, Three, and Eir provide competitive packages that include data, local calls, and texts. These SIM cards can be used in unlocked phones and are a convenient way to stay connected throughout your trip. For extended stays, consider getting a local plan that offers better value for money and more extensive coverage.

When planning your trip, check if your accommodation offers reliable internet, especially if you need to work remotely. Using apps like TripAdvisor or Booking.com, you can filter options by Wi-Fi availability and read reviews about connectivity quality. Additionally, investing in a portable Wi-Fi device can be a good backup, ensuring you have internet access wherever you go. Always have a list of places with free Wi-Fi, such as cafes and libraries, in case you need to find a spot to work or stay connected in an emergency.

Packing Tips for Ireland's Weather

Ireland's weather is famously unpredictable, making versatile packing essential for a comfortable trip. The climate is generally mild but can change rapidly, so layering is key. Lightweight, waterproof outerwear is a must, as rain showers are common year-round. Even in summer, it's wise to pack a mix of short and long sleeves, as temperatures can vary. Including a warm sweater or fleece will ensure you're prepared for cooler evenings and unexpected chills.

Footwear is another important consideration. Comfortable, waterproof walking shoes or boots are ideal for exploring Ireland's cities and countryside. Whether you're hiking the Cliffs of Moher or strolling through Dublin, sturdy footwear will keep you comfortable and dry. A good pair of wellies (rubber boots) can be useful for particularly wet conditions or countryside walks.

Don't forget essentials like an umbrella, a hat, and sunglasses, as well as sunscreen to protect against UV rays, which can still be strong even on overcast days. For those traveling with electronics, consider bringing a power strip with surge protection and the appropriate plug adapters, as Ireland uses a different plug type and voltage than many other countries. Packing a reusable water bottle and a small daypack will also make day trips and excursions more convenient.

Cultural Etiquette and Local Customs

Understanding Irish cultural etiquette and local customs can enhance your travel experience, helping you connect more meaningfully with locals. The Irish are known for their friendliness and hospitality, often going out of their way to help visitors. Politeness and good manners are highly valued, so simple courtesies like saying "please" and "thank you" go a long way. Engaging in small talk, particularly about the weather, is a common way to break the ice.

When visiting pubs, it's customary to take turns buying rounds of drinks if you're in a group. This practice, known as "getting a round in," is an important part of social etiquette. Tipping is appreciated but not obligatory; rounding up the bill or leaving a small amount is usually sufficient in casual dining settings. In restaurants, a tip of 10-15% is standard for good service.

Respect for local traditions and sites is crucial. When visiting religious sites, such as churches and monasteries, dress modestly and behave respectfully. Many Irish people have a deep connection to their cultural heritage, so showing interest and respect for their history and customs is always appreciated. Attempting a few words of Irish Gaelic, such as "Sláinte" (cheers) or "Dia dhuit" (hello), can also endear you to locals, even if most people primarily speak English.

By embracing these cultural nuances and being prepared for the weather, you'll navigate Ireland more smoothly and enrich your travel experience. This will help you build positive interactions and ensure a respectful and enjoyable visit.

Shopping Tips

Shopping in Ireland offers a delightful blend of traditional crafts, contemporary fashion, and unique souvenirs, making it an integral part of your travel experience. One of the quintessential items to buy in Ireland is Aran knitwear, known for its intricate patterns and quality craftsmanship. These sweaters, scarves, and hats, originally from the Aran Islands, are perfect keepsakes that provide warmth and style. You'll find authentic Aran knitwear in specialty shops across the country, particularly in Dublin and Galway. Another must-buy is Irish linen, celebrated for its fine quality and used in everything from clothing to home décor. Visit stores like Avoca Handweavers for a wide selection of beautifully crafted linen items.

Ireland is also famous for its traditional music instruments, such as bodhráns (Irish drums) and tin whistles. These make excellent gifts for music enthusiasts and are available in music shops like Walton's Music in Dublin. Irish crystal, especially from Waterford, is another luxurious souvenir. Waterford Crystal's factory and retail store in Waterford City offer a range of exquisite crystal pieces, from delicate glassware to ornate chandeliers. Additionally, don't miss out on Irish whiskey, with brands like Jameson, Bushmills, and smaller boutique distilleries providing tours and tastings that can be concluded with the purchase of a bottle to take home.

For those interested in contemporary Irish fashion and design, Dublin's Creative Quarter, spanning South William Street, George's Street, and surrounding areas, is a hub for boutique shopping. Here, you can find unique clothing, jewelry, and home accessories crafted by Irish designers. Shops like Designist and Om Diva showcase the best of Irish creativity. Traditional Irish jewelry, such as Claddagh rings and Celtic knot designs, can be found in reputable stores like Weir & Sons in Dublin and The Cat and The Moon in Sligo. Markets like the English Market in Cork and St. George's Market in Belfast offer an array of local produce, handmade crafts, and delicious food items, providing a rich, immersive shopping experience.

When planning your shopping excursions, consider the following tips to make the most of your time and budget. First, always look for quality and authenticity, particularly with traditional crafts. Stores with good reputations and clear sourcing information are preferable. Second, take advantage of tax-free shopping for non-EU residents, which allows you to reclaim VAT on purchases over a certain amount. Many larger stores and airports offer this service, making it easier to save on your purchases. Lastly, don't hesitate to ask locals for recommendations. They can often point you to hidden gems and local favorites that might not be in the guidebooks, ensuring you have a genuinely unique shopping experience in Ireland.

Final Thoughts

Ireland, with its rich history, vibrant culture, and breathtaking landscapes, offers an unforgettable travel experience. Beyond the well-trodden paths of major cities and tourist hotspots, the true charm of Ireland lies in its hidden gems, local traditions, and the warm hospitality of its people. Whether you are exploring the ancient monastic sites of Glendalough, marveling at the rugged beauty of the Wild Atlantic Way, or immersing yourself in the lively arts scene of Dublin, every corner of Ireland has something unique to offer.

As you journey through Ireland, remember to embrace the spontaneous moments that often turn into the most cherished memories. Take time to engage with the locals, whether in a bustling pub or a quiet village market, as these interactions can provide deeper insights into the Irish way of life. Respect the natural environment by following Leave No Trace principles, ensuring that the stunning landscapes remain pristine for future generations. Additionally, try to learn a few basic phrases in Irish Gaelic; even simple greetings can enhance your cultural connection and show your appreciation for the local heritage.

In preparation for your trip, ensure you are well-equipped for the ever-changing weather by packing versatile clothing and waterproof gear. Make use of local resources, such as visitor centers and online travel forums, to stay informed about events, festivals, and must-see attractions. Ireland's diverse culinary scene, from traditional dishes to contemporary gastronomy, is another aspect not to be missed, offering a delicious exploration of the island's flavors.

Ultimately, your travels in Ireland are not just about the destinations but the journey itself. With its blend of scenic beauty, cultural richness, and welcoming atmosphere, Ireland invites you to discover its soul and create lasting memories. So, embark on this adventure with an open heart and a spirit of curiosity, and let Ireland's magic unfold before you. Safe travels, or as the Irish say, "Slán abhaile" – safe home.

CHAPTER 9:
10 Must-Have Cultural Experiences in Ireland

Ireland's cultural experiences are deeply rooted in its rich history, vibrant traditions, and warm community spirit. This chapter will guide you through ten must-have cultural experiences that will immerse you in the heart of Irish culture. From lively festivals to ancient traditions, each experience offers a unique glimpse into the soul of Ireland. Whether you're a history buff, a music enthusiast, or simply curious about the local way of life, these activities will enrich your journey and create lasting memories.

Attending a Local Festival

Attending a local festival in Ireland is a fantastic way to experience the country's vibrant culture and community spirit. Festivals in Ireland are as diverse as its landscape, ranging from the world-famous St. Patrick's Day celebrations to smaller, local events that honor traditional music, dance, and crafts. Each festival offers a unique blend of activities, performances, and local flavors, making it a must-do experience for visitors.

St. Patrick's Day, celebrated on March 17th, is undoubtedly the most iconic festival, with parades, music, and dance transforming cities and towns across the country. However, there are many other festivals that provide an equally enriching experience. For instance, the Galway International Arts Festival, held every July, showcases an impressive array of visual art, theater, and music. Similarly, the Fleadh Cheoil na hÉireann, an annual traditional Irish music festival, attracts musicians and fans from around the world, offering a week-long celebration of Irish culture.

To make the most of your festival experience, plan your visit around the festival dates and book accommodations early, as these events often attract large crowds. Check local listings and festival websites for schedules and ticket information. Engaging with locals during these events can enhance your experience, providing insights and stories that you won't find in guidebooks. Whether you join in the festive parades, enjoy live music sessions, or sample local delicacies, attending an Irish festival is a memorable way to connect with the culture and people of Ireland.

Exploring a Whiskey Distillery

Exploring a whiskey distillery in Ireland is a journey into the heart of one of the country's most cherished traditions. Irish whiskey, known for its smooth and distinctive flavor, has been crafted here for centuries, with distilleries ranging from large, historic establishments to small, artisanal producers. A visit to a distillery offers not only a taste of this fine spirit but also an insight into the meticulous processes and rich history behind its production.

The Old Jameson Distillery in Dublin and the Midleton Distillery in County Cork are among the most famous, offering comprehensive tours that include guided tastings and a chance to learn about the distillation process. These tours typically start with a historical overview, followed by a walkthrough of the various stages of whiskey production, from malting and mashing to fermentation, distillation, and maturation. At the end of the tour, visitors often get to sample a range of whiskeys, guided by knowledgeable staff who can explain the subtle differences between each variety.

For those looking to explore lesser-known distilleries, places like the Dingle Distillery in County Kerry and the Teeling Distillery in Dublin offer a more intimate experience. These smaller operations often allow visitors to see the distillers at work and ask questions about their craft. To ensure a smooth visit, book your tour in advance, especially during peak tourist seasons. Many distilleries also have gift shops where you can purchase bottles of their finest whiskey, making for a perfect souvenir or gift. Whether you're a whiskey connoisseur or a curious traveler, exploring an Irish whiskey distillery is a fascinating and enjoyable cultural experience.

Participating in a Traditional Irish Music Session

Participating in a traditional Irish music session, or "seisiún," is a quintessential Irish experience that offers a deep dive into the country's musical heritage. These informal gatherings, often held in pubs, bring together local musicians and enthusiasts to play traditional Irish music, creating an atmosphere filled with lively tunes and a sense of camaraderie. The music, typically featuring instruments like the fiddle, tin whistle, uilleann pipes, and bodhrán, ranges from fast-paced jigs and reels to hauntingly beautiful slow airs.

Traditional music sessions can be found throughout Ireland, with some of the most renowned taking place in counties Clare, Galway, and Donegal. Cities like Dublin and Galway are famous for their vibrant music scenes, but smaller towns and villages also offer authentic and memorable sessions. For example, Doolin in County Clare is known for its lively music sessions, attracting musicians and music lovers from around the world.

To fully enjoy a traditional music session, simply visit a local pub known for its live music. You don't need a ticket or reservation, but arriving early ensures a good seat. Listening attentively and clapping along to the music is appreciated, and if you're a musician, bringing your instrument and joining the session is often welcomed. Sessions typically start in the evening and can go on until late at night, creating a cozy and engaging atmosphere. Participating in a traditional Irish music session is not just about the music; it's about experiencing the warmth and hospitality of Irish culture in its most genuine form.

Visiting a Traditional Irish Music Session

Participating in a traditional Irish music session, or "seisiún," is a quintessential Irish experience that offers a deep dive into the country's musical heritage. These informal gatherings, often held in pubs, bring together local musicians and enthusiasts to play traditional Irish music, creating an atmosphere filled with lively tunes and a sense of camaraderie. The music, typically featuring instruments like the fiddle, tin whistle, uilleann pipes, and bodhrán, ranges from fast-paced jigs and reels to hauntingly beautiful slow airs.

Traditional music sessions can be found throughout Ireland, with some of the most renowned taking place in counties

Clare, Galway, and Donegal. Cities like Dublin and Galway are famous for their vibrant music scenes, but smaller towns and villages also offer authentic and memorable sessions. For example, Doolin in County Clare is known for its lively music sessions, attracting musicians and music lovers from around the world.

To fully enjoy a traditional music session, simply visit a local pub known for its live music. You don't need a ticket or reservation, but arriving early ensures a good seat. Listening attentively and clapping along to the music is appreciated, and if you're a musician, bringing your instrument and joining the session is often welcomed. Sessions typically start in the evening and can go on until late at night, creating a cozy and engaging atmosphere. Participating in a traditional Irish music session is not just about the music; it's about experiencing the warmth and hospitality of Irish culture in its most genuine form.

Learning Irish Dance

Learning Irish dance is a vibrant and energetic way to connect with Ireland's rich cultural traditions. Irish dance, characterized by its rapid leg movements and intricate footwork, has gained worldwide fame through performances like Riverdance and Lord of the Dance. Whether you're a novice or an experienced dancer, participating in an Irish dance class or workshop can be a fun and rewarding experience that offers insight into this traditional art form.

Many dance schools across Ireland offer classes for visitors, ranging from beginner lessons to more advanced sessions. Dublin, Cork, and Galway are home to some renowned dance schools where you can learn from skilled instructors. These classes often cover various styles of Irish dance, including step dancing, set dancing, and ceili dancing. Step dancing is known for its solo performances, while set and ceili dancing are social dances performed in groups, making them a great way to meet new people and immerse yourself in the local culture.

For those looking for a more immersive experience, attending an Irish dance festival or competition can provide a deeper appreciation of the skill and dedication involved in this art form. The Fleadh Cheoil na hÉireann, held annually, includes dance competitions and workshops, offering a perfect opportunity to witness and learn Irish dance. When planning to participate, wear comfortable shoes and be ready for an energetic workout. Engaging with Irish dance not only enriches your cultural understanding but also offers a unique and enjoyable way to stay active during your travels.

Touring a Historic Castle

Touring a historic castle in Ireland is like stepping back in time, offering a glimpse into the country's storied past and architectural grandeur. Ireland is home to numerous castles, each with its own unique history and charm. From medieval fortresses to grand estates, these castles provide fascinating insights into Ireland's heritage and the lives of its former inhabitants.

One of the most iconic castles to visit is Dublin Castle, located in the heart of the capital. This historic site has served as a military fortress, royal residence, and government complex over the centuries. Visitors can explore its beautifully preserved state apartments, medieval undercroft, and the Gothic Chapel Royal. Another must-see is Kilkenny Castle, a stunning 12th-century structure surrounded by lush gardens and parklands. Inside, the castle boasts lavishly decorated rooms and an impressive art collection.

For those interested in more off-the-beaten-path experiences, places like Bunratty Castle in County Clare offer a unique blend of history and entertainment. This 15th-century castle hosts medieval banquets, where guests can enjoy a feast accompanied by traditional music and storytelling. Similarly, the Rock of Cashel in County Tipperary provides a dramatic setting with its ancient ruins and panoramic views of the surrounding countryside.

To make the most of your castle tour, check the opening hours and availability of guided tours, as these can provide valuable context and stories behind the architecture and artifacts. Wear comfortable shoes for walking and bring a camera to capture the breathtaking views. Touring a historic castle is not only an educational experience but also a chance to marvel at the architectural splendor and historical significance of these majestic structures.

Participating in a Gaelic Games Experience

Participating in a Gaelic games experience offers a thrilling dive into Ireland's national sports, providing a unique and energetic way to connect with the country's cultural heritage. Gaelic games, including hurling and Gaelic football, are deeply ingrained in Irish culture, boasting a passionate following and a history that spans thousands of years. These fast-paced, skillful sports are overseen by the Gaelic Athletic Association (GAA), which promotes and organizes competitions across the country.

Hurling, often described as the fastest field sport in the world, involves players using a wooden stick called a hurley to hit a small ball, or sliotar, between the opposing team's goalposts. Gaelic football, on the other hand, is a thrilling blend of soccer and rugby, where players can use both their hands and feet to pass and score. Both sports are known for their speed, skill, and physicality, making them exhilarating to watch and play.

To truly experience the excitement of Gaelic games, consider attending a match at Croke Park in Dublin, the headquarters of the GAA and one of the largest stadiums in Europe. Here, you can witness the electrifying atmosphere of championship matches, particularly during the All-Ireland finals held in September. For a more hands-on experience, many local GAA clubs offer visitors the chance to participate in training sessions or introductory workshops. These sessions are designed to teach the basic skills and rules of the games, providing a fun and interactive way to engage with Irish sports culture.

When planning your Gaelic games experience, check the GAA website for match schedules and club information. Attending a live match requires tickets, which can be purchased online or at the stadium. For workshops and training sessions, contacting local GAA clubs directly will provide the best options. Participating in Gaelic games not only offers an adrenaline-pumping activity but also immerses you in a beloved aspect of Irish life, connecting you with the heart of the community.

Exploring Irish Folklore and Mythology

Exploring Irish folklore and mythology opens a window into a world filled with enchanting tales, legendary heroes, and mystical creatures that have shaped Ireland's cultural identity for centuries. Ireland's rich oral tradition is replete with stories of fairies, banshees, leprechauns, and ancient gods, each woven into the fabric of the nation's history and landscapes. These myths and legends offer fascinating insights into the beliefs and values of the Irish people, providing a deeper understanding of their cultural heritage.

One of the most famous cycles of Irish mythology is the Ulster Cycle, which features the epic tales of Cú Chulainn, a legendary warrior known for his superhuman feats and tragic destiny. Another key cycle is the Mythological Cycle, which recounts the stories of ancient gods and the mythical invasions of Ireland. The Fenian Cycle, focusing on the hero Fionn mac Cumhaill and his band of warriors, the Fianna, is also central to Irish folklore. These tales are not only captivating but also reflect the moral and social values of ancient Irish society.

To delve into Irish folklore and mythology, consider visiting sites that are steeped in legend. The Hill of Tara in County Meath, once the seat of the High Kings of Ireland, is a place of great historical and mythological significance. Newgrange, a prehistoric monument in the Boyne Valley, is another key site associated with ancient myths. Additionally, the National Leprechaun Museum in Dublin offers an interactive journey through Ireland's folklore, bringing these enchanting stories to life.

For a more immersive experience, participating in guided tours that focus on Irish mythology can provide deeper insights and engaging narratives. Storytelling sessions, often held in traditional pubs or cultural centers, are also a wonderful way to experience the magic of Irish folklore. Exploring these tales through books, such as Lady Gregory's "Gods and Fighting Men" or Thomas Kinsella's "The Táin," can further enhance your understanding. Engaging with Irish folklore and mythology allows you to connect with Ireland's ancient past and the timeless stories that continue to inspire its people.

Visiting Literary Landmarks

Visiting literary landmarks in Ireland is a journey through the rich tapestry of the country's literary heritage, offering a glimpse into the lives and works of some of the world's most celebrated writers. Ireland has produced a remarkable number of influential authors, poets, and playwrights, whose works have left an indelible mark on literature. From the lyrical prose of James Joyce to the haunting poetry of W.B. Yeats, Ireland's literary tradition is as diverse as it is profound.

Dublin, a UNESCO City of Literature, is a literary hub where many of these famous writers lived and worked. Trinity College Dublin, home to the stunning Old Library and the Book of Kells, is a must-visit for literature enthusiasts. The Dublin Writers Museum offers an overview of the country's literary history, featuring exhibits on Joyce, Yeats, and Samuel Beckett, among others. A visit to the James Joyce Centre provides insights into the life of the author of "Ulysses," with exhibits and walking tours that explore the Dublin locations immortalized in his works.

Beyond Dublin, Ireland is dotted with literary landmarks. In Sligo, you can visit the Yeats Memorial Building and explore the landscapes that inspired W.B. Yeats' poetry. The Seamus Heaney HomePlace in Bellaghy, Northern Ireland, celebrates the life and work of the Nobel Prize-winning poet. In County Clare, you can explore Thoor Ballylee, the tower house that Yeats called home for many years. Literary festivals, such as the Dublin International Literature Festival and the Listowel Writers' Week, provide opportunities to celebrate and engage with Irish literature.

To make the most of your literary pilgrimage, consider joining guided tours that focus on Ireland's literary heritage. These tours often include visits to significant sites, readings, and expert commentary, enriching your understanding of the country's literary landscape. Additionally, attending literary events and festivals can provide unique opportunities to connect with contemporary Irish writers and explore the ongoing literary tradition. Visiting these literary landmarks allows you to step into the world of Ireland's literary giants and appreciate the enduring legacy of their works.

Experiencing the Gaeltacht Regions

Experiencing the Gaeltacht regions of Ireland offers a unique glimpse into the country's linguistic and cultural heritage, where the Irish language (Gaeilge) is still widely spoken in daily life. These regions, located primarily along the western seaboard, are not only linguistic strongholds but also cultural heartlands where traditional Irish music, dance, and folklore are deeply embedded in community life. Visiting the Gaeltacht is like stepping back in time to experience a way of life that has remained largely unchanged for centuries.

The most renowned Gaeltacht areas include Connemara in County Galway, the Dingle Peninsula in County Kerry, and the Aran Islands off the coast of Galway. These regions are characterized by their stunning natural landscapes, from rugged coastlines and windswept islands to rolling hills and boglands. In Connemara, you can explore the picturesque villages, visit local markets, and enjoy the hospitality of traditional Irish pubs where live music sessions are a regular feature. The Dingle Peninsula offers a mix of dramatic scenery and vibrant cultural life, with opportunities to attend language classes and cultural workshops. The Aran Islands, with their ancient forts and monastic sites, provide a serene and enriching cultural immersion.

Engaging with the local community is key to fully appreciating the Gaeltacht experience. Many regions offer language immersion courses, providing an excellent opportunity to learn or improve your Irish language skills. Cultural festivals, such as the Oireachtas na Gaeilge, celebrate Irish language and arts through competitions in storytelling, singing, and dancing. Staying in local B&Bs or with host families can enhance your understanding of the daily life and traditions of the Gaeltacht communities.

When visiting the Gaeltacht, consider joining a guided tour that focuses on the cultural and linguistic heritage of the area. These tours often include visits to historical sites, participation in traditional music sessions, and opportunities to converse with native Irish speakers. Supporting local businesses and artisans by purchasing handmade crafts and attending cultural events also helps sustain the vibrant heritage of these regions. Experiencing the Gaeltacht is a profound way to connect with Ireland's cultural roots and enrich your understanding of its enduring traditions.

Learning the Art of Irish Baking

Learning the art of Irish baking provides a delicious and engaging way to immerse yourself in Ireland's culinary traditions. Irish baking is renowned for its hearty and comforting creations, from traditional soda bread and scones to rich fruit cakes and buttery pastries. These baked goods are a staple of Irish cuisine, often enjoyed with a cup of tea or as part of a traditional Irish breakfast. Exploring the world of Irish baking offers a hands-on way to connect with the country's culinary heritage and bring a taste of Ireland into your own kitchen.

Traditional Irish soda bread, made with just a few simple ingredients such as flour, baking soda, buttermilk, and salt, is a quintessential part of Irish baking. This bread is known for its dense texture and slightly tangy flavor, making it a perfect accompaniment to soups and stews. Scones, another staple, are light and fluffy, often studded with raisins or currants and served with clotted cream and jam. Irish fruit cake, rich with dried fruits and spices, is a festive treat enjoyed during holidays and special occasions.

To learn the art of Irish baking, consider enrolling in a baking class or workshop. Many culinary schools and local bakeries across Ireland offer hands-on classes where you can learn to bake traditional Irish recipes under the guidance of experienced bakers. These classes often include a historical overview of the recipes, tips on sourcing the best ingredients, and techniques for achieving the perfect bake. Attending a baking class not only hones your skills but also provides a delightful way to meet fellow baking enthusiasts and share your creations.

For those unable to attend a class in person, numerous online resources and cookbooks are available to guide you through the process. Websites dedicated to Irish cuisine often feature step-by-step recipes and video tutorials, making it easy to follow along from the comfort of your own kitchen. Exploring local bakeries and cafes during your travels in Ireland can also offer inspiration and a deeper appreciation for the traditional baking methods and flavors. Learning the art of Irish baking is a rewarding and enjoyable way to savor the rich culinary traditions of Ireland and share them with friends and family.

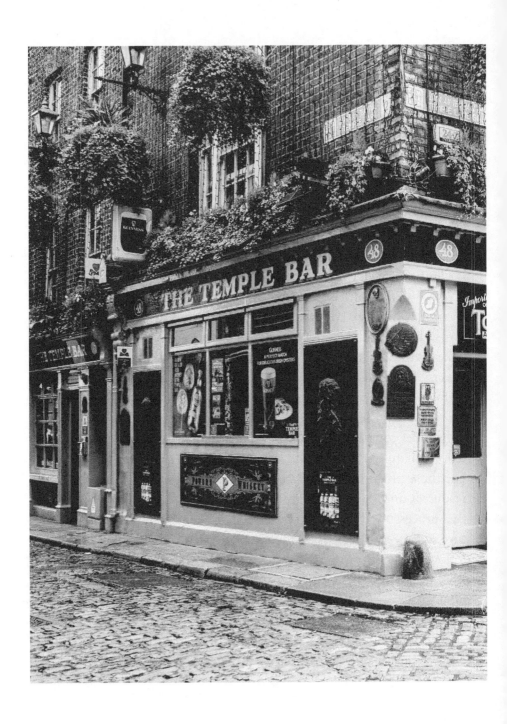

CHAPTER 10:
Recommended Itinerary for a 10-Day Stay

Planning a 10-day trip to Ireland is an adventure filled with rich history, stunning landscapes, and vibrant culture. This itinerary will guide you through some of the country's most iconic destinations and hidden gems, ensuring you experience the best that Ireland has to offer. From the bustling streets of Dublin to the serene beauty of the Wild Atlantic Way and the ancient sites of the Boyne Valley, this journey will leave you with unforgettable memories and a deep appreciation for the Emerald Isle.

When planning your trip to Ireland, consider the best time to visit, which typically falls between April and September, when the weather is milder and the days are longer. Ensure you have all necessary travel documents, including a valid passport and any required visas. Booking accommodations and transportation in advance is advisable, especially during peak tourist seasons. Renting a car is a popular option for exploring Ireland, giving you the flexibility to travel at your own pace and visit off-the-beaten-path locations. Make sure to pack appropriately for Ireland's unpredictable weather, with layers and waterproof clothing being essential.

DAY 1-2: Arrival and Exploring Dublin

Upon arriving in Dublin, the capital city of Ireland, you'll be greeted with a blend of historic charm and modern vibrancy. Start your exploration with a visit to Trinity College, home to the renowned Book of Kells, an illuminated manuscript dating back to the 9th century. Wander through the college's beautiful library, which houses an impressive collection of ancient texts and is an architectural marvel in its own right.

Next, head to the Guinness Storehouse, where you can learn about the history of Ireland's most famous stout. The seven-story visitor experience culminates in the Gravity Bar, offering panoramic views of Dublin while you enjoy a complimentary pint of Guinness. Continue your journey with a visit to Dublin Castle, a historic fortress that has played a pivotal role in Ireland's history. Explore the State Apartments, the Chapel Royal, and the medieval undercroft.

In the evening, immerse yourself in Dublin's lively nightlife in the Temple Bar District. Known for its cobblestone streets and vibrant atmosphere, this area is filled with traditional pubs, live music venues, and eclectic eateries. Be sure to sample some local dishes and enjoy a pint of Irish ale while listening to live traditional Irish music.

DAY 3-4: The Wild Atlantic Way

Embark on a scenic drive along the Wild Atlantic Way, a 2,500-kilometer coastal route that stretches from the Inishowen Peninsula in Donegal to Kinsale in County Cork. Begin your journey at the Cliffs of Moher, where you can walk along the towering cliffs and enjoy breathtaking views of the Atlantic

Ocean. Continue to the Dingle Peninsula, known for its rugged beauty, ancient sites, and charming villages. Take the Slea Head Drive, a loop that offers stunning coastal views and passes by landmarks such as Gallarus Oratory and Dunbeg Fort. Spend the night in Dingle town, where you can enjoy fresh seafood and traditional Irish music in the local pubs.

On Day 4, head south to the Ring of Kerry, a famous circular route that showcases the best of County Kerry's landscapes. Highlights include Killarney National Park, with its beautiful lakes and mountains, and the picturesque villages of Kenmare and Sneem. Take your time to explore the scenic viewpoints, such as Ladies View and Moll's Gap, and consider taking a boat trip to Skellig Michael, a UNESCO World Heritage Site known for its early Christian monastery and stunning sea views.

DAY 5: Galway City and Connemara

Travel to Galway City, a vibrant cultural hub known for its lively atmosphere, colorful streets, and historic sites. Stroll through the Latin Quarter, visit the Galway City Museum, and enjoy the buskers and street performers that add to the city's charm. Don't miss the Spanish Arch and Eyre Square, two of the city's iconic landmarks.

In the afternoon, head to Connemara National Park, renowned for its rugged landscapes, bogs, and mountains. Explore the park's walking trails, which offer spectacular views of the Twelve Bens mountain range and the Atlantic coastline. Visit Kylemore Abbey, a stunning Gothic Revival castle set against a backdrop of wooded hills and a reflective lake. The abbey's Victorian Walled Garden is also worth exploring.

DAY 6-7: The Ancient East

Journey to Ireland's Ancient East, a region rich in history and heritage. Start with a visit to Glendalough, a monastic site nestled in the Wicklow Mountains. Explore the ancient ruins, including the round tower and St. Kevin's Church, and take a walk around the scenic lakes.

Continue to Kilkenny, known for its well-preserved medieval buildings and vibrant arts scene. Visit Kilkenny Castle, stroll through the medieval streets, and explore the artisan shops and cafes. Don't miss the Medieval Mile Museum, which offers insights into Kilkenny's history.

On Day 7, visit the Rock of Cashel, a dramatic hilltop fortress that was once the seat of the Kings of Munster. Explore the ancient cathedral, round tower, and Cormac's Chapel. Next, head to Waterford, Ireland's oldest city, known for its Viking history and Waterford Crystal. Take a tour of the Waterford Crystal factory and visit the Viking Triangle, a cultural and heritage area that includes Reginald's Tower and the Medieval Museum.

DAY 8: Northern Ireland's Highlights

Cross into Northern Ireland to explore some of its top attractions. Start with a visit to the Giant's Causeway, a UNESCO World Heritage Site known for its unique hexagonal basalt columns. Learn about the geological and mythical origins of this natural wonder at the visitor center.

Next, head to Titanic Belfast, an award-winning museum that tells the story of the RMS Titanic, from its construction to its ill-fated maiden voyage. The interactive exhibits and full-scale reconstructions provide a fascinating insight into the ship's history.

Finish the day with a visit to Carrick-a-Rede Rope Bridge, a thrilling suspension bridge that spans a 30-meter deep chasm. Enjoy the stunning coastal views and watch for seabirds and marine life.

DAY 9: Hidden Gems and Scenic Drives

Spend your penultimate day exploring some of Ireland's hidden gems and taking scenic drives through lesser-known but equally beautiful areas. Start with a visit to the Slieve League Cliffs in County Donegal, which are among the highest sea cliffs in Europe. The views from the top are spectacular, and there are several walking trails for different fitness levels.

Next, drive through the Burren, a unique karst landscape in County Clare known for its limestone pavements, rare flora, and ancient monuments. Stop by the Poulnabrone Dolmen, a prehistoric portal tomb, and explore the Burren Perfumery and its beautiful herb gardens.

End the day with a drive along the Beara Peninsula, a less-touristed but stunningly scenic area in County Cork and County Kerry. The Ring of Beara offers rugged coastal views, charming villages, and ancient stone circles. Consider stopping in the towns of Allihies and Castletownbere for a taste of local life.

DAY 10: Departure or Extended Stay Options

On your final day, depending on your departure time, you can explore more of Dublin or nearby attractions. Visit the National Museum of Ireland or take a leisurely walk through

Phoenix Park. If you have more time, consider extending your stay to explore additional regions such as the Midlands or the Sunny Southeast.

For those interested in an extended stay, options include a visit to the Aran Islands for a taste of traditional Irish culture and stunning landscapes, or a trip to the Shannon region to explore Bunratty Castle and Folk Park. Whatever you choose, make sure to take some time to reflect on the incredible journey and the memories you've made along the way.

Other Itinerary Options

While the 10-day itinerary offers a comprehensive overview of Ireland's highlights, there are countless other ways to explore the Emerald Isle. For history enthusiasts, consider starting your journey in Dublin, spending two days diving into its rich past with visits to Dublin Castle, Trinity College, the Book of Kells, Kilmainham Gaol, and the National Museum of Ireland. From there, a day in the Boyne Valley exploring Newgrange, Knowth, and the Hill of Tara is a must. Following this, spend two days in Kilkenny and Cashel to see Kilkenny Castle, St. Canice's Cathedral, and the iconic Rock of Cashel. A day in Waterford will allow you to tour the famous Waterford Crystal Factory and the Viking Triangle. Finally, wrap up your historical journey with two days in Cork and Blarney, visiting the English Market, Blarney Castle, and the charming town of Cobh.

For nature lovers, Dublin and Wicklow offer a perfect blend of city and nature with Phoenix Park, Dublin Zoo, and the scenic beauty of Glendalough. Then, head to Killarney and the Ring of Kerry for two days to enjoy Killarney National Park, Muckross House, and a stunning scenic drive. Spend a day hiking in the

Burren and walking along the Cliffs of Moher before moving on to Connemara for two days to visit Kylemore Abbey and explore Connemara National Park. Conclude your nature-focused trip with three days in Donegal and the North Coast, where you can hike the Slieve League Cliffs, explore Glenveagh National Park, and marvel at the Giant's Causeway.

For those interested in culture and cuisine, begin with three days in Dublin to enjoy literary tours, traditional music sessions, and pub crawls. Spend two days in Cork visiting the English Market, Jameson Distillery, and enjoying a seafood feast in Kinsale. Next, two days in Galway will immerse you in the city's vibrant arts scene, traditional music, and Claddagh ring history. A day in Limerick and Clare will allow you to visit the Hunt Museum, King John's Castle, and enjoy a medieval banquet at Bunratty Castle. Finally, wrap up with two days in Northern Ireland, touring Belfast's Titanic Quarter, enjoying a whiskey tasting at Bushmills, and exploring the mystical Dark Hedges.

These alternative itineraries offer a variety of ways to experience Ireland, whether you're drawn to its rich history, breathtaking nature, or vibrant culture and cuisine. Each journey promises unique experiences and unforgettable memories, ensuring that your time in Ireland is as enriching and enjoyable as possible.

Conclusion

Ireland, with its rich history, vibrant culture, and stunning landscapes, offers an unforgettable experience for every traveler. Throughout this guide, we have explored the multifaceted beauty of the Emerald Isle, from the bustling streets of Dublin to the serene countryside retreats, providing you with a comprehensive roadmap for an enriching journey. Each chapter has highlighted different aspects of Ireland, inviting you to immerse yourself in its charm and heritage.

Exploring Ireland is about more than just visiting its famous landmarks; it's about connecting with its spirit. Whether you're standing on the edge of the Cliffs of Moher, listening to traditional music in a cozy pub, or walking through the ancient streets of Kilkenny, Ireland provides a feast for the senses and the soul. This country is not merely a destination but a journey into a culture that values storytelling, community, and a deep connection to the land.

The essence of Ireland lies in its people. The Irish are renowned for their warmth, hospitality, and wit. Engaging with locals—whether by participating in a Gaelic games experience, visiting a traditional music session, or sharing stories over a pint of Guinness—provides insights into their way of life that go beyond typical tourist experiences. This cultural immersion enriches your visit, leaving you with a deeper appreciation for Ireland's heritage and values.

For digital nomads, Ireland offers an inspiring blend of productivity and leisure. The island's growing network of coworking spaces, coupled with its picturesque landscapes and vibrant expatriate community, creates an ideal environment for remote work. Whether you're setting up your laptop in a bustling Dublin café or a tranquil space in Galway, the balance of work and play is effortlessly achieved in Ireland.

Respecting local customs and the environment is crucial to preserving Ireland's beauty. Embrace sustainable travel practices by choosing eco-friendly accommodations, supporting local businesses, and minimizing your environmental footprint. Engage in activities that promote conservation and cultural preservation, such as guided tours of historical sites or participating in local festivals. By doing so, you contribute positively to Ireland's future while enhancing your own experience.

To make your journey smoother and more engaging, here are some useful Irish phrases:

▷ "Dia dhuit" – Hello

▷ "Go raibh maith agat" – Thank you

▷ "Le do thoil" – Please

▷ "Cé mhéad atá air?" – How much does it cost?

▷ "Cá bhfuil an leithreas?" – Where is the bathroom?

▷ "Is ainm dom…" – My name is…

▷ "An féidir leat cabhrú liom?" – Can you help me?

▷ "Caife, le do thoil" – Coffee, please

▷ "Maidin mhaith" – Good morning

▷ "Oíche mhaith" – Good night

▷ "Ní labhraím Gaeilge go maith" – I don't speak much Irish

▷ "Cá bhfuil...?" – Where is...?

▷ "Ba mhaith liom..." – I would like...

▷ "Tá mé caillte" – I'm lost

Your time in Ireland will be filled with moments of wonder and discovery. Whether you're exploring the vibrant markets of Dublin, relaxing on the beaches of the Wild Atlantic Way, trekking through the lush hills of the Wicklow Mountains, or diving into the rich literary heritage of the island, each experience adds a unique thread to the tapestry of your journey.

Embrace Ireland's spirit of hospitality and openness. Allow yourself to be moved by its natural beauty, inspired by its cultural depth, and connected by its sense of community. Travel not just to see new places but to grow, learn, and become part of the world in a more profound way.

As you reflect on your travels, remember that the true beauty of Ireland lies not just in its landscapes but in the moments of connection and understanding that you experience along the way. Here's to the adventures that await you, the friendships you'll forge, and the memories you'll cherish long after you leave the island's shores.

Slán abhaile (safe travels) and enjoy every moment of your Irish adventure. Ireland is more than a destination; it's a journey of the heart and soul, a place where you can find peace, inspiration, and a deeper connection to the world around you.

Made in the USA
Las Vegas, NV
06 December 2024

13465816R00094